The Life Planner:

Discovering Yourself
and Achieving Your Goals

by

Laura Huber

TELEMACHUS
PRESS

The Life Planner: Discovering Yourself and Achieving Your Goals

Cover art and design by Telemachus Press, LLC
Cover Art Photo iStockphoto #17361713/Woman Silhouette against Spectacular Mountain Panorama/Marco Maccarini

Published by Telemachus Press, LLC
http://www.telemachuspress.com

ISBN# 978-1-937698-62-1

Version 2011.12.05

Printed in the United States of America

10 9 8 7 6 5 4 3 2 1

This book is dedicated to everyone who wishes to become and achieve everything they desire.

The Life Planner:

Discovering Yourself
and Achieving Your Goals

In order for you to "Discover yourself, and Achieve your goals," you MUST <u>read this section first and do each and every step!</u>

<u>Step #1. Ask yourself the question: Who?</u>

Who do you want to be? Maybe you want to be just like your great aunt. Maybe you want to be like *Time* magazine's person of the year, Mark Zuckerberg. Maybe you want to be like your son's Bible school teacher. There is no wrong answer. Just remember to always be a first rate impression of yourself, and not a second rate someone else. Make a list of the kind of qualities you admire in others, and the kind of person you dream of being. Try to think of twelve qualities and work on one each month. By the end of this year you'll be much closer to **who** you want to be. Always start by writing it like you've already achieved it. Your words have tremendous power. Try saying things in a very positive way, and believe in yourself. Sometimes your goals change. This is normal. Change desires when necessary and write them in the spaces for extra notes.
Example:
1. <u>I am **patient** and **kind**.</u>
2. <u>I always know the right thing to say.</u>
3. <u>I am wise, and use my **wisdom** to help mankind.</u>

Now it's your turn. Try it.

1._____

2._____

3._____

4._____

5._____

6._____

7._____

8._____

9._____

10._____

11._____

12._____

Extra notes:

_____

_____

_____

_____

_____

_____

Step #2. Ask yourself the question: What?

What do you want to achieve? Make sure there are things on this list that will make you grow as a person. It will be easy achieving things to make others' lives more desirable. Like, making sure your children are learning about wonderful and interesting things and making sure your home runs smoothly, but what are some things that you want to achieve for yourself? Would you like to learn to play the piano? Learn calligraphy? Maybe, you're like me and enjoy reading, writing and teaching and want to share it with the world. If I can do it – you can do it. All you have to do is write down your desires, and believe. Remember the words of Jesus, "Believe that you have already received it, and it will be yours." Now is not the time to become too humble to accept the desires that God is whispering in your heart. Those desires are there for a reason. Make sure you hear them. Then make sure you go on to achieve them. Desire without action is just wishful thinking.

Remember everything builds on something else. You will learn many more things when you break out of your comfort zone and try something new. Life is much more fun once you decide to do this. Now, grab a cup of hot tea. Find a quiet, comfy spot. Breathe deeply, and ask the Holy Spirit to speak to you about the things God wants for **YOU**. Write down three things that will impact you and your family and three things that will impact only you.
Example:

1. My house is always clean and tidy.
2. I always know what 's for supper each night.
3. Our family goes on a fun outing every month.

1. I am a successful author, making $50K monthly
2. I have purchased 1,000 acres of land to teach people how to respect and preserve the earth.
3. I can now speak Spanish, French and German.

Now it's your turn. Try it.

1. _____
   _____

2. _____
   _____

3. _____
   _____

1. _____
   _____

2. _____
   _____

3. _____
   _____

Extra notes:

_____
_____
_____
_____
_____
_____

Step #3. Ask yourself the question: When?

When do you want to achieve the things you've listed on the last two pages? Use the space provided at the end of each month section to decide when you want to achieve each goal. This is **when** action really comes into play. Maybe you want your house to always be clean and tidy starting right now, but it isn't possible with the methods you and your family have been using lately. You need to think of an action plan to get the ball rolling. Maybe you could download the "Duty Directory" from my website www.laurahuber.com this might be your first step. Remember everything is much easier with the right tools. So think of what you'll need to help make **when** happen sooner and not later.

Example:

1. HOUSE: Look up Duty Directory. Assign each person a room per week to be responsible for cleaning and maintaining. Buy some disposable cleaning clothes for each room. House clean and re-organize one room per month.

2. SUPPER: Set aside time on Sunday night to make menu for week. Go shopping every Monday to make sure everything is readily available.

3. OUTINGS: Since #1 and #2 are achieved - this is easier. Make a list of things everyone wants to do and choose one each week.

1. Author: Set aside time to start writing. Look up just what other authors do to become successful. Find a publisher. Create a website. Advertise.

Now it's your turn. You try it:

_____

_____

_____

_____

_____

_____

_____

_____

_____

_____

_____

_____

_____

_____

_____

_____

_____

_____

_____

_____

_____

_____

Step #4. Ask yourself the question: Where?

Where does all of your time go? If you don't have a plan, precious seconds, minutes, hours, and even days and months go slipping through our hands like the sands of time in an hour glass. So figure out **where** you want all your time to go by filling out the charts on the next pages. There is one for each season.

Example for your daily routine:

AM	SUN	MON	TUES	WED	THUR	FRI	SAT
12:00	Sleep	Sleep	Sleep	Sleep	Sleep	Sleep	Sleep
1:00							
2:00							
3:00							
4:00							
5:00							
6:00		Get up, start day. Shower, write	Get up, start day. Shower, write	Get up, start day. Shower, write	Get up, start day. Shower, write	Get up, start day Shower, write	
7:00	Get up, start day. Church	Write and read. laundry	Write and read	Write and read. laundry	Write and read	Write and read. laundry	Get up, start day. shower
8:00		Breakfast wake kids laundry	Breakfast wake kids	Breakfast wake kids laundry	Breakfast wake kids	Breakfast wake kids laundry	Curl hair do nails
9:00	Breakfast, read, relax	Write more and clean	Make calls and clean	Write more and clean	Make calls and clean	Write more and clean	
10:00		Begin teaching school	Begin teaching school	Begin teaching school	Begin teaching school	Begin teaching school	
11:00		school	school	school	school	School, movies, games	

Note to homeschoolers: Children are working on school on their own from 8:30 until their assignments are finished. After kids finish, I work with them one on one for as long as needed. Usually we finish around 1:00 pm.

*This chart could be for the fall season. For me that is the day after Labor Day until sometime in November, depending on weather. Notice, there are places which are not filled in. This is very important to allow yourself some free time. Fill these places up with spur of the moment, pleasant pleasures or extra time to achieve goals. Remember **you** decide how to live your life. Only fill in one season's schedule at a time. At the beginning of each season, re-evaluate to decide what is best for your life at that time.

PM	SUN	MON	TUES	WED	THUR	FRI	SAT
12:00		school	school	school	school		
1:00		Lunch, clean up, laundry	Lunch, clean up, laundry	Lunch, clean up, laundry	Lunch, clean up, laundry	Lunch and have fun	
2:00		Home caring, laundry	Home caring, gardening	Home caring, laundry	Scheduled appoint-ments		
3:00	Soft ball games	bake something	Shopping	Yard work			
4:00							
5:00							
6:00		Start supper	Start supper	Start supper	Start supper	Soccer practice	Baseball games
7:00		Baseball practice	Soccer games			Pizza night	
8:00		Sit down and eat together	Sit down and eat together	Sit down and eat together	Sit down and eat together	Sit down and eat together	
9:00							
10:00							
11:00	bedtime	bedtime	bedtime	bedtime	bedtime		

Now it's your turn. You give it a try: Use this one for **WINTER.**

AM	SUN	MON	TUES	WED	THUR	FRI	SAT
12:00							
1:00							
2:00							
3:00							
4:00							
5:00							
6:00							
7:00							
8:00							
9:00							
10:00							
11:00							

PM	SUN	MON	TUES	WED	THUR	FRI	SAT
12:00							
1:00							
2:00							
3:00							
4:00							
5:00							
6:00							
7:00							
8:00							
9:00							
10:00							
11:00							

Use this one for **SPRING:**

AM	SUN	MON	TUES	WED	THUR	FRI	SAT
12:00							
1:00							
2:00							
3:00							
4:00							
5:00							
6:00							
7:00							
8:00							
9:00							
10:00							
11:00							

PM	SUN	MON	TUES	WED	THUR	FRI	SAT
12:00							
1:00							
2:00							
3:00							
4:00							
5:00							
6:00							
7:00							
8:00							
9:00							
10:00							
11:00							

Use this one for **SUMMER:**

AM	SUN	MON	TUES	WED	THUR	FRI	SAT
12:00							
1:00							
2:00							
3:00							
4:00							
5:00							
6:00							
7:00							
8:00							
9:00							
10:00							
11:00							

PM	SUN	MON	TUES	WED	THUR	FRI	SAT
12:00							
1:00							
2:00							
3:00							
4:00							
5:00							
6:00							
7:00							
8:00							
9:00							
10:00							
11:00							

Use this one for **FALL:**

AM	SUN	MON	TUES	WED	THUR	FRI	SAT
12:00							
1:00							
2:00							
3:00							
4:00							
5:00							
6:00							
7:00							
8:00							
9:00							
10:00							
11:00							

PM	SUN	MON	TUES	WED	THUR	FRI	SAT
12:00							
1:00							
2:00							
3:00							
4:00							
5:00							
6:00							
7:00							
8:00							
9:00							
10:00							
11:00							

Step #5. Ask yourself the question: How?

How are you going to spend your days? **How** are you going to accomplish your goals for this year? Just ahead are the pages that are going to make it work. Before you begin each month, write down important events such as birthdays, anniversaries, or scheduled appointments for the year. Fill in as needed.

A monthly example:

JANUARY

1 Party with Mom's family
2
3
4 Aunt Lou's birthday
5
6 Take down Christmas decorations
7
8
9 Jackie and Kevin's anniversary

Next, figure out the night before, or early the next day, **five** things that must be accomplished to make it a prosperous day. Yes, everyone has more than five things that must be accomplished each day, but if you write down more than that you will feel overwhelmed. If you don't get Monday's goals completed on Monday, you will feel like you're already behind when Tuesday morning starts fresh and new. The key is to accomplish what you have written down. This gives you a feeling of achievement, which will soon make all the difference in your life. If you get more than five things finished you may write a few more in the places marked with a **(*)**. These are bonuses.

A daily example:

TODAY'S DATE: January 12, 2012

Be not afraid of going slowly, be afraid of standing still.

Chinese proverb

MY GOALS FOR TODAY:	CALLS AND CONTACTS TO MAKE TODAY:
1. 4 loads of laundry	bank
2. work on my closet	Telemachus Press
3. Go to library – Appalachia	IMI Software
4. Pay bills	
5. Build snowman with kids	SCHEDULED EVENTS AND REMINDERS:
*	Kristin – volley ball practice @6:00
*	Call Beth tomorrow
*	
*	
FOR SUPPER TONIGHT WE'LL HAVE: Pork chops, fried apples, mashed potatoes and gravy.	
MY GOALS FOR THIS WEEK:	MY GOALS FOR THIS MONTH:
House clean my bedroom, and straighten my closet.	Completely go over house and clean and straighten every room

Notice you don't have to list everything you do each day, just the things you want to make sure to complete. Your daily routine pages help keep you on track with all the other things you must do each day.

Remember to write down what your goals are for each week and every month. Chunk down your bigger goals into smaller ones and do something daily to get you closer to the desired results.

Every other day you will write down the "**ULTIMATE GOAL**." This is your largest goal. You have one year to make it happen. I cannot stress enough how important it is to write down your goals every day.

A daily example: (*from opposite side*)

TODAY'S DATE: <u>August 12, 2011</u>

A minute's success pays the failure of years.

Robert Browning

MY GOALS FOR TODAY:	CALLS AND CONTACTS TO MAKE TODAY:
1. yoga	Aunt Beth
2. House cleaned	
3. Grass mowed	
4. Sheets washed	
5. School books ordered	SCHEDULED EVENTS AND REMINDERS:
*	Mom's birthday
*	
*	
*	
FOR SUPPER TONIGHT WE'LL HAVE: Roast beef, mashed potatoes, corn	
MY ULTIMATE GOAL FOR THIS YEAR: To publish the ABC's of Home Schooling, and market it well. Selling over 100,000 copies.	NOTES: New website ideas: Recipe page, blogging, etc.

The places at the bottom of each daily page may be tempting to skip, but by writing down the things you want to accomplish each and every day – be they large or small – you are turning on a switch in your sub-conscience mind to help you achieve them.

Try it for one year.

Be diligent.

Only good things can come out of this experiment.

After each month page there are only enough daily pages available to write down goals for five days per week. Two days are left for you to dream, imagine and rest. This is a very important part of achieving anything, because we all know too well the feeling of being, "burned out." Take time to rest and do some of the fun suggestions listed on the month pages. Not only will you create some wonderful memories for yourself — and those you love, but you will be recharged and excited to start working after resting.

There are two extra pages tucked in every month for really busy weeks; just make sure to take a couple days off each week when possible.

After completing each task, cross it off with a red, fine tipped marker. I don't know why, but this feels really good.

If you accomplish only five goals per day, five days a week, and you accomplish one big goal per week, one major goal per month, and one ultimate goal for the year, you will have achieved **1,364 goals**. You will be able to look back over the year with a wonderful sense of accomplishment, and be proud of what you've done. (There are instructions in back to help you accomplish larger goals.)

Only one step left – **BEGIN**!

What is that one thing that you really want to accomplish this year? Write it down on the next page, and then work to make it happen.

Remember always the words of Rabindranath Tagore, who received the 1913 Nobel laureate for literature:

"You can't cross a sea by merely staring into the water."

It's time for you to start living the life of your dreams. Grab a pen and start planning.

MY ULTIMATE GOAL FOR THIS YEAR IS:

_____

_____

_____

_____

_____

_____

_____

JANUARY

New, white, crisp, and clean – days are brighter than they seem.
It's time for everyone to make a fresh start.
What are the dreams hidden deep in your heart?
Today's the day to write them down. If you do, success will be found.

1	
2	
3	
4	
5	
6	
7	
8	
9	
10	
11	
12	
13	
14	
15	
16	
17	
18	
19	
20	
21	

22	
23	
24	
25	
26	
27	
28	
29	
30	
31	

FUN THINGS TO DO THIS MONTH:

1. If you have snow on the ground. Try something new. Paint a snowman using water colored with food coloring and spray bottles.
2. Buy some marshmallows, chocolate bars, and graham crackers. Build a fire inside or out and make some s'mores.
3. Lie on your back in the snow. Look up at the beauty of nature. While you're down there, make a snow angel.
4. Go for a winter hike. This is especially "cool" when the trees are wrapped in ice.
5. Collect some interesting magazines and begin a "Creative Discovery Journal." Do this by cutting out pictures you are drawn to and pasting them in a binder with loose leaf paper; you'll soon know just what it is you want in life.

MUST DO THIS MONTH

1. Write down your ultimate goal for this year on designated page.
2. I will work on this character trait during January.

_____

3. I will work on these goals this month:

_____

_____

TODAY'S DATE _____

Be not afraid of going slowly, be afraid of standing still.

Chinese proverb

MY GOALS FOR TODAY:	CALLS AND CONTACTS TO MAKE TODAY:
1.	
2.	
3.	
4.	
5.	SCHEDULED EVENTS AND REMINDERS:
*	
*	
*	
*	
FOR SUPPER TONIGHT WE'LL HAVE:	
MY GOALS FOR THIS WEEK:	MY GOALS FOR THIS MONTH:

TODAY'S DATE _____

A minute's success pays the failure of years.

Robert Browning

MY GOALS FOR TODAY:	CALLS AND CONTACTS TO MAKE TODAY:
1.	
2.	
3.	
4.	
5.	SCHEDULED EVENTS AND REMINDERS:
*	
*	
*	
*	
FOR SUPPER TONIGHT WE'LL HAVE:	
MY ULTIMATE GOAL FOR THIS YEAR:	NOTES:

TODAY'S DATE _____

Grace in women has more effect than beauty.

William Hazlitt

MY GOALS FOR TODAY:	CALLS AND CONTACTS TO MAKE TODAY:
1.	
2.	
3.	
4.	
5.	SCHEDULED EVENTS AND REMINDERS:
*	
*	
*	
*	
FOR SUPPER TONIGHT WE'LL HAVE:	
MY GOALS FOR THIS WEEK:	MY GOALS FOR THIS MONTH:

TODAY'S DATE_____

You have no cause for anything but gratitude and joy.

Gautama Buddha

MY GOALS FOR TODAY:	CALLS AND CONTACTS TO MAKE TODAY:
1.	
2.	
3.	
4.	
5.	SCHEDULED EVENTS AND REMINDERS:
*	
*	
*	
*	
FOR SUPPER TONIGHT WE'LL HAVE:	
MY ULTIMATE GOAL FOR THIS YEAR:	NOTES:

TODAY'S DATE_____

*Never give up, for that is just the place and
time that the tide will turn.*

Harriet Beecher Stowe

MY GOALS FOR TODAY:	CALLS AND CONTACTS TO MAKE TODAY:
1.	
2.	
3.	
4.	
5.	SCHEDULED EVENTS AND REMINDERS:
*	
*	
*	
*	
FOR SUPPER TONIGHT WE'LL HAVE:	
MY GOALS FOR THIS WEEK:	MY GOALS FOR THIS MONTH:

TODAY'S DATE_____

*Happiness is like an old friend, is inclined to drop in
unexpectedly — when you're working hard on something else. . .*

Ray Inman

MY GOALS FOR TODAY:	CALLS AND CONTACTS TO MAKE TODAY:
1.	
2.	
3.	
4.	
5.	SCHEDULED EVENTS AND REMINDERS:
*	
*	
*	
*	
FOR SUPPER TONIGHT WE'LL HAVE:	
MY ULTIMATE GOAL FOR THIS YEAR:	NOTES:

TODAY'S DATE_____

A wise man will make more opportunities than he finds.

Francis Bacon

MY GOALS FOR TODAY:	CALLS AND CONTACTS TO MAKE TODAY:
1.	
2.	
3.	
4.	
5.	SCHEDULED EVENTS AND REMINDERS:
*	
*	
*	
*	
FOR SUPPER TONIGHT WE'LL HAVE:	
MY GOALS FOR THIS WEEK:	MY GOALS FOR THIS MONTH:

TODAY'S DATE _____

Without enthusiasm, every task is difficult . . .

Anonymous

MY GOALS FOR TODAY:	CALLS AND CONTACTS TO MAKE TODAY:
1.	
2.	
3.	
4.	
5.	SCHEDULED EVENTS AND REMINDERS:
*	
*	
*	
*	
FOR SUPPER TONIGHT WE'LL HAVE:	
MY ULTIMATE GOAL FOR THIS YEAR:	NOTES:

TODAY'S DATE_____

When a man's willing and eager, God joins in . . .

Aeschylus

MY GOALS FOR TODAY:	CALLS AND CONTACTS TO MAKE TODAY:
1.	
2.	
3.	
4.	
5.	SCHEDULED EVENTS AND REMINDERS:
*	
*	
*	
*	
FOR SUPPER TONIGHT WE'LL HAVE:	
MY GOALS FOR THIS WEEK:	MY GOALS FOR THIS MONTH:

TODAY'S DATE_____

Work is love made visible.

Khalil Gibran

MY GOALS FOR TODAY:	CALLS AND CONTACTS TO MAKE TODAY:
1.	
2.	
3.	
4.	
5.	SCHEDULED EVENTS AND REMINDERS:
*	
*	
*	
*	
FOR SUPPER TONIGHT WE'LL HAVE:	
MY ULTIMATE GOAL FOR THIS YEAR:	NOTES:

TODAY'S DATE _____

Men will always delight in a woman whose voice is lined with velvet.

Brendan Francis

MY GOALS FOR TODAY:	CALLS AND CONTACTS TO MAKE TODAY:
1.	
2.	
3.	
4.	
5.	SCHEDULED EVENTS AND REMINDERS:
*	
*	
*	
*	
FOR SUPPER TONIGHT WE'LL HAVE:	
MY GOALS FOR THIS WEEK:	MY GOALS FOR THIS MONTH:

TODAY'S DATE _____

*If you don't know where you're going,
you'll end up sleeping someplace else.*

Yogi Berra

MY GOALS FOR TODAY:	CALLS AND CONTACTS TO MAKE TODAY:
1.	
2.	
3.	
4.	
5.	SCHEDULED EVENTS AND REMINDERS:
*	
*	
*	
*	
FOR SUPPER TONIGHT WE'LL HAVE:	
MY ULTIMATE GOAL FOR THIS YEAR:	NOTES:

TODAY'S DATE _____

The seed never explains the flower.

Edith Hamilton

MY GOALS FOR TODAY:	CALLS AND CONTACTS TO MAKE TODAY:
1.	
2.	
3.	
4.	
5.	SCHEDULED EVENTS AND REMINDERS:
*	
*	
*	
*	
FOR SUPPER TONIGHT WE'LL HAVE:	
MY GOALS FOR THIS WEEK:	MY GOALS FOR THIS MONTH:

TODAY'S DATE _____

With blessing everything is possible. . .

Rabindranath Tagore

MY GOALS FOR TODAY:	CALLS AND CONTACTS TO MAKE TODAY:
1.	
2.	
3.	
4.	
5.	SCHEDULED EVENTS AND REMINDERS:
*	
*	
*	
*	
FOR SUPPER TONIGHT WE'LL HAVE:	
MY ULTIMATE GOAL FOR THIS YEAR:	NOTES:

TODAY'S DATE_____

The most common way people give up their power is by thinking they don't have any.

Alice Walker

MY GOALS FOR TODAY:	CALLS AND CONTACTS TO MAKE TODAY:
1.	
2.	
3.	
4.	
5.	SCHEDULED EVENTS AND REMINDERS:
*	
*	
*	
*	
FOR SUPPER TONIGHT WE'LL HAVE:	
MY GOALS FOR THIS WEEK:	MY GOALS FOR THIS MONTH:

TODAY'S DATE_____

When a thing bores you, do not do it.
Do not pursue fruitless perfection . . .

Eugene Delacroix

MY GOALS FOR TODAY:	CALLS AND CONTACTS TO MAKE TODAY:
1.	
2.	
3.	
4.	
5.	SCHEDULED EVENTS AND REMINDERS:
*	
*	
*	
*	
FOR SUPPER TONIGHT WE'LL HAVE:	
MY ULTIMATE GOAL FOR THIS YEAR:	NOTES:

TODAY'S DATE _____

Just don't give up trying to do what you really want to do. Where there is love and inspiration I don't think you can go wrong.

Ella Fitzgerald

MY GOALS FOR TODAY:	CALLS AND CONTACTS TO MAKE TODAY:
1.	
2.	
3.	
4.	
5.	SCHEDULED EVENTS AND REMINDERS:
*	
*	
*	
*	
FOR SUPPER TONIGHT WE'LL HAVE:	
MY GOALS FOR THIS WEEK:	MY GOALS FOR THIS MONTH:

TODAY'S DATE _____

A wise woman puts a grain of sugar into everything she says to a man and takes a grain of salt with everything a man says to her.

Helen Rowland

MY GOALS FOR TODAY:	CALLS AND CONTACTS TO MAKE TODAY:
1.	
2.	
3.	
4.	
5.	SCHEDULED EVENTS AND REMINDERS:
*	
*	
*	
*	
FOR SUPPER TONIGHT WE'LL HAVE:	
MY ULTIMATE GOAL FOR THIS YEAR:	NOTES:

TODAY'S DATE_____

You take your life into your own hands, and what happens?
A terrible thing: no one to blame.

Erica Jong

MY GOALS FOR TODAY:	CALLS AND CONTACTS TO MAKE TODAY:
1.	
2.	
3.	
4.	
5.	SCHEDULED EVENTS AND REMINDERS:
*	
*	
*	
*	
FOR SUPPER TONIGHT WE'LL HAVE:	
MY GOALS FOR THIS WEEK:	MY GOALS FOR THIS MONTH:

TODAY'S DATE _____

A man who cannot tolerate small ills
can never accomplish great things . . .

Chinese proverb

MY GOALS FOR TODAY:	CALLS AND CONTACTS TO MAKE TODAY:
1.	
2.`	
3.	
4.	
5.	SCHEDULED EVENTS AND REMINDERS:
*	
*	
*	
*	
FOR SUPPER TONIGHT WE'LL HAVE:	
MY ULTIMATE GOAL FOR THIS YEAR:	NOTES:

TODAY'S DATE_____

When it is obvious that goals cannot be reached,
don't adjust the goals, adjust the action steps.

Confucius

MY GOALS FOR TODAY:	CALLS AND CONTACTS TO MAKE TODAY:
1.	
2.	
3.	
4.	
5.	SCHEDULED EVENTS AND REMINDERS:
*	
*	
*	
*	
FOR SUPPER TONIGHT WE'LL HAVE:	
MY GOALS FOR THIS WEEK:	MY GOALS FOR THIS MONTH:

TODAY'S DATE_____

Set your course by the stars,
not by the lights of every passing ship.

Omar Bradley

MY GOALS FOR TODAY:	CALLS AND CONTACTS TO MAKE TODAY:
1.	
2.	
3.	
4.	
5.	SCHEDULED EVENTS AND REMINDERS:
*	
*	
*	
*	
FOR SUPPER TONIGHT WE'LL HAVE:	
MY ULTIMATE GOAL FOR THIS YEAR:	NOTES:

♥ FEBRUARY ♥

Valentines and love's sweet gifts,
hearts are warm while white snow drifts.
Red velvet cake is fun to make.
It smells delicious while it bakes.
Send heart shaped notes to loved ones far,
to let them know how special they are.

1	
2	
3	
4	
5	
6	
7	
8	
9	
10	
11	
12	
13	
14	
15	
16	
17	
18	
19	
20	

21	
22	
23	
24	
25	
26	
27	
28	
29	

FUN THINGS TO DO THIS MONTH:

1. Ask yourself, "What is it I truly love?" Trust in the answers that come, and your authentic life will unfold naturally.
2. February 2 is Candlemas Day. At dusk turn off all the lights and enjoy the peaceful gentle flames.
3. Buy a red tablecloth and some white doilies. To make Valentine's Day unforgettable, do like my mother, and decorate the doilies for each individual who will be dining with you on February 14th.
4. There are many different myths about how Valentine's Day began. My favorite is: St. Valentine was imprisoned. He fell in love with the jailor's daughter. One day while she was visiting, he slipped her a note declaring his love, and signed it, "Your Valentine." Make your own Valentines by cutting vintage pictures from last year's Christmas cards and gluing them on pretty paper. Send them to someone special.
5. Force some spring bulbs. Kids **love** this.

MUST DO THIS MONTH

1. I will work on this character trait during February.

   _____

2. I will work on these goals this month:

   _____

TODAY'S DATE_____

The world is but a canvas to our imaginations . . .

Henry D. Thoreau

MY GOALS FOR TODAY:	CALLS AND CONTACTS TO MAKE TODAY:
1.	
2.	
3.	
4.	
5.	SCHEDULED EVENTS AND REMINDERS:
*	
*	
*	
*	
FOR SUPPER TONIGHT WE'LL HAVE:	
MY GOALS FOR THIS WEEK:	MY GOALS FOR THIS MONTH:

TODAY'S DATE_____

There is no right or wrong. There is only love. . .

Carol Chapman

MY GOALS FOR TODAY:	CALLS AND CONTACTS TO MAKE TODAY:
1.	
2.	
3.	
4.	
5.	SCHEDULED EVENTS AND REMINDERS:
*	
*	
*	
*	
FOR SUPPER TONIGHT WE'LL HAVE:	
MY ULTIMATE GOAL FOR THIS YEAR:	NOTES:

TODAY'S DATE_____

Life shrinks or expands according to one's courage.
Anais Nin

MY GOALS FOR TODAY:	CALLS AND CONTACTS TO MAKE TODAY:
1.	
2.	
3.	
4.	
5.	SCHEDULED EVENTS AND REMINDERS:
*	
*	
*	
*	
FOR SUPPER TONIGHT WE'LL HAVE:	
MY GOALS FOR THIS WEEK:	MY GOALS FOR THIS MONTH:

TODAY'S DATE _____

Miracles only happen to the people who believe in them.

Anonymous

MY GOALS FOR TODAY:	CALLS AND CONTACTS TO MAKE TODAY:
1.	
2.	
3.	
4.	
5.	SCHEDULED EVENTS AND REMINDERS:
*	
*	
*	
*	
FOR SUPPER TONIGHT WE'LL HAVE:	
MY ULTIMATE GOAL FOR THIS YEAR:	NOTES:

TODAY'S DATE _____

The only limit put on choice is that it cannot serve two masters.

A Course in Miracles

MY GOALS FOR TODAY:	CALLS AND CONTACTS TO MAKE TODAY:
1.	
2.	
3.	
4.	
5.	SCHEDULED EVENTS AND REMINDERS:
*	
*	
*	
*	
FOR SUPPER TONIGHT WE'LL HAVE:	
MY GOALS FOR THIS WEEK:	MY GOALS FOR THIS MONTH:

TODAY'S DATE _____

How we spend our days, is of course, how we spend our lives.

Annie Dillard

MY GOALS FOR TODAY:	CALLS AND CONTACTS TO MAKE TODAY:
1.	
2.	
3.	
4.	
5.	SCHEDULED EVENTS AND REMINDERS:
*	
*	
*	
*	
FOR SUPPER TONIGHT WE'LL HAVE:	
MY ULTIMATE GOAL FOR THIS YEAR:	NOTES:

TODAY'S DATE _____

Normal day, let me be aware of the treasure you are. Let me not pass you by in some quest of some rare and perfect tomorrow.

Mary Jean Irion

MY GOALS FOR TODAY:	CALLS AND CONTACTS TO MAKE TODAY:
1.	
2.	
3.	
4.	
5.	SCHEDULED EVENTS AND REMINDERS:
*	
*	
*	
*	
FOR SUPPER TONIGHT WE'LL HAVE:	
MY GOALS FOR THIS WEEK:	MY GOALS FOR THIS MONTH:

TODAY'S DATE _____

*Our deepest wishes are whispers of authentic selves. We must
learn to respect them. We must learn to listen.*

Sarah Ban Breathnach

MY GOALS FOR TODAY:	CALLS AND CONTACTS TO MAKE TODAY:
1.	
2.	
3.	
4.	
5.	SCHEDULED EVENTS AND REMINDERS:
*	
*	
*	
*	
FOR SUPPER TONIGHT WE'LL HAVE:	
MY ULTIMATE GOAL FOR THIS YEAR:	NOTES:

TODAY'S DATE _____

People with clenched fists cannot shake hands.

Indira Gandhi

MY GOALS FOR TODAY:	CALLS AND CONTACTS TO MAKE TODAY:
1.	
2.	
3.	
4.	
5.	SCHEDULED EVENTS AND REMINDERS:
*	
*	
*	
*	
FOR SUPPER TONIGHT WE'LL HAVE:	
MY GOALS FOR THIS WEEK:	MY GOALS FOR THIS MONTH:

TODAY'S DATE _____

Don't bunt. Aim out of the ballpark.

David Ogilvy

MY GOALS FOR TODAY:	CALLS AND CONTACTS TO MAKE TODAY:
1.	
2.	
3.	
4.	
5.	SCHEDULED EVENTS AND REMINDERS:
*	
*	
*	
*	
FOR SUPPER TONIGHT WE'LL HAVE:	
MY ULTIMATE GOAL FOR THIS YEAR:	NOTES:

TODAY'S DATE _____

There are two things to aim for in life; first to get what you want, and after that enjoy it. Only the wisest of mankind has achieved the second.

Logan Pearsall Smith

MY GOALS FOR TODAY:	CALLS AND CONTACTS TO MAKE TODAY:
1.	
2.	
3.	
4.	
5.	SCHEDULED EVENTS AND REMINDERS:
*	
*	
*	
*	
FOR SUPPER TONIGHT WE'LL HAVE:	
MY GOALS FOR THIS WEEK:	MY GOALS FOR THIS MONTH:

TODAY'S DATE _____

You have everything. You are the whole world. Why?
Because the kingdom of God is within you.
Then why do you want to run about and beg?

Yogi Swami

MY GOALS FOR TODAY:	CALLS AND CONTACTS TO MAKE TODAY:
1.	
2.	
3.	
4.	
5.	SCHEDULED EVENTS AND REMINDERS:
*	
*	
*	
*	
FOR SUPPER TONIGHT WE'LL HAVE:	
MY ULTIMATE GOAL FOR THIS YEAR:	NOTES:

TODAY'S DATE _____

Most people are standing on a pile of gold looking at a pile of silver in the distance. . .

Anonymous

MY GOALS FOR TODAY:	CALLS AND CONTACTS TO MAKE TODAY:
1.	
2.	
3.	
4.	
5.	SCHEDULED EVENTS AND REMINDERS:
*	
*	
*	
*	
FOR SUPPER TONIGHT WE'LL HAVE:	
MY GOALS FOR THIS WEEK:	MY GOALS FOR THIS MONTH:

TODAY'S DATE _____

Seek ye first the kingdom of God, and his righteousness,
and all things will be given to you.

Jesus

MY GOALS FOR TODAY:	CALLS AND CONTACTS TO MAKE TODAY:
1.	
2.	
3.	
4.	
5.	SCHEDULED EVENTS AND REMINDERS:
*	
*	
*	
*	
FOR SUPPER TONIGHT WE'LL HAVE:	
MY ULTIMATE GOAL FOR THIS YEAR:	NOTES:

TODAY'S DATE _____

The future depends on what we do in the present.

Mahatma Gandhi

MY GOALS FOR TODAY:	CALLS AND CONTACTS TO MAKE TODAY:
1.	
2.	
3.	
4.	
5.	SCHEDULED EVENTS AND REMINDERS:
*	
*	
*	
*	
FOR SUPPER TONIGHT WE'LL HAVE:	
MY GOALS FOR THIS WEEK:	MY GOALS FOR THIS MONTH:

TODAY'S DATE _____

Pray to God but continue to row the boat to shore . . .

Russian proverb

MY GOALS FOR TODAY:	CALLS AND CONTACTS TO MAKE TODAY:
1.	
2.	
3.	
4.	
5.	SCHEDULED EVENTS AND REMINDERS:
*	
*	
*	
*	
FOR SUPPER TONIGHT WE'LL HAVE:	
MY ULTIMATE GOAL FOR THIS YEAR:	NOTES:

TODAY'S DATE _____

What lies behind us and what lies before us are tiny matters compared to what lies within us.

Oliver W. Holmes

MY GOALS FOR TODAY:	CALLS AND CONTACTS TO MAKE TODAY:
1.	
2.	
3.	
4.	
5.	SCHEDULED EVENTS AND REMINDERS:
*	
*	
*	
*	
FOR SUPPER TONIGHT WE'LL HAVE:	
MY GOALS FOR THIS WEEK:	MY GOALS FOR THIS MONTH:

TODAY'S DATE _____

No one can build his security
upon the nobleness of another person.

Willa Cather

MY GOALS FOR TODAY:	CALLS AND CONTACTS TO MAKE TODAY:
1.	
2.	
3.	
4.	
5.	SCHEDULED EVENTS AND REMINDERS:
*	
*	
*	
*	
FOR SUPPER TONIGHT WE'LL HAVE:	
MY ULTIMATE GOAL FOR THIS YEAR:	NOTES:

TODAY'S DATE _____

He who is being carried does not realize
how far the next town is.

African proverb

MY GOALS FOR TODAY:	CALLS AND CONTACTS TO MAKE TODAY:
1.	
2.	
3.	
4.	
5.	SCHEDULED EVENTS AND REMINDERS:
*	
*	
*	
*	
FOR SUPPER TONIGHT WE'LL HAVE:	
MY GOALS FOR THIS WEEK:	MY GOALS FOR THIS MONTH:

TODAY'S DATE _____

I give people what they want,
so eventually they'll want what I have to give.

Shirdi Sai Baba

MY GOALS FOR TODAY:	CALLS AND CONTACTS TO MAKE TODAY:
1.	
2.	
3.	
4.	
5.	SCHEDULED EVENTS AND REMINDERS:
*	
*	
*	
*	
FOR SUPPER TONIGHT WE'LL HAVE:	
MY ULTIMATE GOAL FOR THIS YEAR:	NOTES:

TODAY'S DATE _____

What is not started today is never finished tomorrow.

Jimmy Dean

MY GOALS FOR TODAY:	CALLS AND CONTACTS TO MAKE TODAY:
1.	
2.	
3.	
4.	
5.	SCHEDULED EVENTS AND REMINDERS:
*	
*	
*	
*	
FOR SUPPER TONIGHT WE'LL HAVE:	
MY GOALS FOR THIS WEEK:	MY GOALS FOR THIS MONTH:

TODAY'S DATE _____

To aim is not enough, you must hit!

Proverb

MY GOALS FOR TODAY:	CALLS AND CONTACTS TO MAKE TODAY:
1.	
2.	
3.	
4.	
5.	SCHEDULED EVENTS AND REMINDERS:
*	
*	
*	
*	
FOR SUPPER TONIGHT WE'LL HAVE:	
MY ULTIMATE GOAL FOR THIS YEAR:	NOTES:

MARCH

March's wind is strong and fast, but winter now is almost past.
It's time for sleeping life to emerge. Go out and spot a migrating bird.
Easter's just around the bend. Springtime comes to us once again.

1	
2	
3	
4	
5	
6	
7	
8	
9	
10	
11	
12	
13	
14	
15	
16	
17	
18	
19	
20	
21	
22	

23	
24	
25	
26	
27	
28	
29	
30	
31	

FUN THINGS TO DO THIS MONTH:

1. Go for a walk in your yard or a nearby nursery. Find some bare branches of any trees or bushes with full and pretty blooms. Apple, cherry, forsythia, etc. Cut the ends at a *slant* and place them in water. Sit in a sunny spot and watch spring burst forth in a bounteous array.

2. Serve a special St. Patrick's Day meal of cooked cabbage, sausage and creamy mashed potatoes. Wash it down with a frosty mug of root beer.

3. Tell your children the story of St. Patrick.

4. Celebrate the first day of spring by planting some pansies or primroses.

5. Two weeks before Easter, plant a living Easter basket. Buy a liner to fit the basket or line it with plastic wrap. Add a couple inches of potting soil, sprinkle with rye or grass seed. Cover with soil. Water carefully. Place in a brown paper bag for a few days. Then bring the basket out. Sit in a sunny location. Water as needed. You may even have to cut grass before Easter. Kids love to this with their own scissors.

6. Read, *The Secret Garden*, and then create one of your own in your *Discovery Journal*. (Suggested in January.) It's easy with old seed catalogs.

MUST DO THIS MONTH

1. I will work on this character trait in March.

_____

2. I will work on these goals this month:

_____

TODAY'S DATE _____

In actual life every great enterprise begins with
and takes its first forward step in faith . . .

August von Schlegel

MY GOALS FOR TODAY:	CALLS AND CONTACTS TO MAKE TODAY:
1.	
2.	
3.	
4.	
5.	SCHEDULED EVENTS AND REMINDERS:
*	
*	
*	
*	
FOR SUPPER TONIGHT WE'LL HAVE:	
MY GOALS FOR THIS WEEK:	MY GOALS FOR THIS MONTH:

TODAY'S DATE _____

The exterior man may be undergoing trials,
but the interior man is quite free.

Meister Eckhart

MY GOALS FOR TODAY:	CALLS AND CONTACTS TO MAKE TODAY:
1.	
2.	
3.	
4.	
5.	SCHEDULED EVENTS AND REMINDERS:
*	
*	
*	
*	
FOR SUPPER TONIGHT WE'LL HAVE:	
MY ULTIMATE GOAL FOR THIS YEAR:	NOTES:

TODAY'S DATE _____

A woman is like a tea bag – you never know how strong she is until she gets in hot water.

Eleanor Roosevelt

MY GOALS FOR TODAY:	CALLS AND CONTACTS TO MAKE TODAY:
1.	
2.	
3.	
4.	
5.	SCHEDULED EVENTS AND REMINDERS:
*	
*	
*	
*	
FOR SUPPER TONIGHT WE'LL HAVE:	
MY GOALS FOR THIS WEEK:	MY GOALS FOR THIS MONTH:

TODAY'S DATE _____

An archeologist is the best husband any woman can have;
the older she gets, the more interested he is in her.

Agatha Christie

MY GOALS FOR TODAY:	CALLS AND CONTACTS TO MAKE TODAY:
1.	
2.	
3.	
4.	
5.	SCHEDULED EVENTS AND REMINDERS:
*	
*	
*	
*	
FOR SUPPER TONIGHT WE'LL HAVE:	
MY ULTIMATE GOAL FOR THIS YEAR:	NOTES:

TODAY'S DATE _____

Never play another person's game. Play your own.

Andrew Salter

MY GOALS FOR TODAY:	CALLS AND CONTACTS TO MAKE TODAY:
1.	
2.	
3.	
4.	
5.	SCHEDULED EVENTS AND REMINDERS:
*	
*	
*	
*	
FOR SUPPER TONIGHT WE'LL HAVE:	
MY GOALS FOR THIS WEEK:	MY GOALS FOR THIS MONTH:

TODAY'S DATE _____

The purpose of life is a life of purpose.

Robert Byrne

MY GOALS FOR TODAY:	CALLS AND CONTACTS TO MAKE TODAY:
1.	
2.	
3.	
4.	
5.	SCHEDULED EVENTS AND REMINDERS:
*	
*	
*	
*	
FOR SUPPER TONIGHT WE'LL HAVE:	
MY ULTIMATE GOAL FOR THIS YEAR:	NOTES:

TODAY'S DATE _____

Yesterday's the past, tomorrow's the future, but today is a gift.
That's why it's called the present.

Bil Keane

MY GOALS FOR TODAY:	CALLS AND CONTACTS TO MAKE TODAY:
1.	
2.	
3.	
4.	
5.	SCHEDULED EVENTS AND REMINDERS:
*	
*	
*	
*	
FOR SUPPER TONIGHT WE'LL HAVE:	
MY GOALS FOR THIS WEEK:	MY GOALS FOR THIS MONTH:

TODAY'S DATE _____

It is easier to produce ten volumes of philosophical writings than to put one principle into practice. . .

Leo Tolstoy

MY GOALS FOR TODAY:	CALLS AND CONTACTS TO MAKE TODAY:
1.	
2.	
3.	
4.	
5.	SCHEDULED EVENTS AND REMINDERS:
*	
*	
*	
*	
FOR SUPPER TONIGHT WE'LL HAVE:	
MY ULTIMATE GOAL FOR THIS YEAR:	NOTES:

TODAY'S DATE _____

Live well, learn plenty, laugh often, love much.

Ralph Waldo Emerson

MY GOALS FOR TODAY:	CALLS AND CONTACTS TO MAKE TODAY:
1.	
2.	
3.	
4.	
5.	SCHEDULED EVENTS AND REMINDERS:
*	
*	
*	
*	
FOR SUPPER TONIGHT WE'LL HAVE:	
MY GOALS FOR THIS WEEK:	MY GOALS FOR THIS MONTH:

TODAY'S DATE _____

Service is the rent we pay for our place on earth . . .

Anonymous

MY GOALS FOR TODAY:	CALLS AND CONTACTS TO MAKE TODAY:
1.	
2.	
3.	
4.	
5.	SCHEDULED EVENTS AND REMINDERS:
*	
*	
*	
*	
FOR SUPPER TONIGHT WE'LL HAVE:	
MY ULTIMATE GOAL FOR THIS YEAR:	NOTES:

TODAY'S DATE _____

In solitude we give passionate attention to our lives,
to our memories, to the details around us.

Virginia Woolf

MY GOALS FOR TODAY:	CALLS AND CONTACTS TO MAKE TODAY:
1.	
2.	
3.	
4.	
5.	SCHEDULED EVENTS AND REMINDERS:
*	
*	
*	
*	
FOR SUPPER TONIGHT WE'LL HAVE:	
MY GOALS FOR THIS WEEK:	MY GOALS FOR THIS MONTH:

TODAY'S DATE _____

The biggest gap in your life is between what you know
and what you do.

Bob Proctor

MY GOALS FOR TODAY:	CALLS AND CONTACTS TO MAKE TODAY:
1.	
2.	
3.	
4.	
5.	SCHEDULED EVENTS AND REMINDERS:
*	
*	
*	
*	
FOR SUPPER TONIGHT WE'LL HAVE:	
MY ULTIMATE GOAL FOR THIS YEAR:	NOTES:

TODAY'S DATE _____

Life itself can be very simple;
it is we who insist on making life complicated. . .

Anonymous

MY GOALS FOR TODAY:	CALLS AND CONTACTS TO MAKE TODAY:
1.	
2.	
3.	
4.	
5.	SCHEDULED EVENTS AND REMINDERS:
*	
*	
*	
*	
FOR SUPPER TONIGHT WE'LL HAVE:	
MY GOALS FOR THIS WEEK:	MY GOALS FOR THIS MONTH:

TODAY'S DATE _____

Your diamonds are not in far distant mountains or in yonder
seas; they are in your own backyard, if you but dig for them.

Russell H. Conwell

MY GOALS FOR TODAY:	CALLS AND CONTACTS TO MAKE TODAY:
1.	
2.	
3.	
4.	
5.	SCHEDULED EVENTS AND REMINDERS:
*	
*	
*	
*	
FOR SUPPER TONIGHT WE'LL HAVE:	
MY ULTIMATE GOAL FOR THIS YEAR:	NOTES:

TODAY'S DATE _____

Seek not outside yourself, heaven is within.

Mary Lou Cook

MY GOALS FOR TODAY:	CALLS AND CONTACTS TO MAKE TODAY:
1.	
2.	
3.	
4.	
5.	SCHEDULED EVENTS AND REMINDERS:
*	
*	
*	
*	
FOR SUPPER TONIGHT WE'LL HAVE:	
MY GOALS FOR THIS WEEK:	MY GOALS FOR THIS MONTH:

TODAY'S DATE _____

It is your work in life that is the ultimate seduction.

Pablo Picasso

MY GOALS FOR TODAY:	CALLS AND CONTACTS TO MAKE TODAY:
1.	
2.	
3.	
4.	
5.	SCHEDULED EVENTS AND REMINDERS:
*	
*	
*	
*	
FOR SUPPER TONIGHT WE'LL HAVE:	
MY ULTIMATE GOAL FOR THIS YEAR:	NOTES:

TODAY'S DATE _____

The greatest of all virtues is to be cheerful . . .

Robert L. Stevenson

MY GOALS FOR TODAY:	CALLS AND CONTACTS TO MAKE TODAY:
1.	
2.	
3.	
4.	
5.	SCHEDULED EVENTS AND REMINDERS:
*	
*	
*	
*	
FOR SUPPER TONIGHT WE'LL HAVE:	
MY GOALS FOR THIS WEEK:	MY GOALS FOR THIS MONTH:

TODAY'S DATE _____

Only when we are no longer afraid do we begin to live.

Dorothy Thompson

MY GOALS FOR TODAY:	CALLS AND CONTACTS TO MAKE TODAY:
1.	
2.	
3.	
4.	
5.	SCHEDULED EVENTS AND REMINDERS:
*	
*	
*	
*	
FOR SUPPER TONIGHT WE'LL HAVE:	
MY ULTIMATE GOAL FOR THIS YEAR:	NOTES:

TODAY'S DATE _____

Fall seven times, stand up eight.

Japanese proverb

MY GOALS FOR TODAY:	CALLS AND CONTACTS TO MAKE TODAY:
1.	
2.	
3.	
4.	
5.	SCHEDULED EVENTS AND REMINDERS:
*	
*	
*	
*	
FOR SUPPER TONIGHT WE'LL HAVE:	
MY GOALS FOR THIS WEEK:	MY GOALS FOR THIS MONTH:

TODAY'S DATE _____

Believe that you shall receive and you shall receive . . .

Jesus

MY GOALS FOR TODAY:	CALLS AND CONTACTS TO MAKE TODAY:
1.	
2.	
3.	
4.	
5.	SCHEDULED EVENTS AND REMINDERS:
*	
*	
*	
*	
FOR SUPPER TONIGHT WE'LL HAVE:	
MY ULTIMATE GOAL FOR THIS YEAR:	NOTES:

TODAY'S DATE _____

You must work; we must all work,
to make the world worthy of its children.

Pablo Casals

MY GOALS FOR TODAY:	CALLS AND CONTACTS TO MAKE TODAY:
1.	
2.	
3.	
4.	
5.	SCHEDULED EVENTS AND REMINDERS:
*	
*	
*	
*	
FOR SUPPER TONIGHT WE'LL HAVE:	
MY GOALS FOR THIS WEEK:	MY GOALS FOR THIS MONTH:

TODAY'S DATE_____

*Fortune knocks but once, but misfortune
has a lot more patience.*

Laurence Peter

MY GOALS FOR TODAY:	CALLS AND CONTACTS TO MAKE TODAY:
1.	
2.	
3.	
4.	
5.	SCHEDULED EVENTS AND REMINDERS:
*	
*	
*	
*	
FOR SUPPER TONIGHT WE'LL HAVE:	
MY GOALS FOR THIS WEEK:	MY GOALS FOR THIS MONTH:

APRIL

If April showers bring May-flowers, what do May-flowers bring?
Pilgrims. It's a joke so you must laugh.
April Fool's Day is a blast.
Do something funny and you'll see, just how happy life can be.

1	
2	
3	
4	
5	
6	
7	
8	
9	
10	
11	
12	
13	
14	
15	
16	
17	
18	
19	
20	
21	

22	
23	
24	
25	
26	
27	
28	
29	
30	

FUN THINGS TO DO THIS MONTH:

1. April Fool's Day can be a day of just plain fun. Do some funny things together, like playing charades. You could even get in a history lesson by only acting out people you've recently studied.
2. With all the unsettled weather this month is a good time to begin scrapbooking. Buy a scrap book for each of your children. Craft stores have an incredible amount of items to choose from.
3. Pick or buy some daffodils use them as a centerpiece for your dining room table.
4. Clean out a closet or just one junk drawer. Wipe down a cabinet. This will get you in the mood for more spring cleaning.
5. Make a batch of hot cross buns on Good Friday.
6. Color some eggs. Let the kids help.
7. Arbor Day is April 22. On this date in 1872, Nebraska planted one million trees across her prairies. Maybe you could just plant one.
8. This is a good month to start a wildflower collection.

MUST DO THIS MONTH

1. I will work on this character trait in April.

_____

2. I will work on these goals this month:

_____

TODAY'S DATE _____

Trust yourself. You know more than you think you do.

Benjamin Spock

MY GOALS FOR TODAY:	CALLS AND CONTACTS TO MAKE TODAY:
1.	
2.	
3.	
4.	
5.	SCHEDULED EVENTS AND REMINDERS:
*	
*	
*	
*	
FOR SUPPER TONIGHT WE'LL HAVE:	
MY GOALS FOR THIS WEEK:	MY GOALS FOR THIS MONTH:

TODAY'S DATE _____

Laughter is inner jogging.

Norman Cousins

MY GOALS FOR TODAY:	CALLS AND CONTACTS TO MAKE TODAY:
1.	
2.	
3.	
4.	
5.	SCHEDULED EVENTS AND REMINDERS:
*	
*	
*	
*	
FOR SUPPER TONIGHT WE'LL HAVE:	
MY ULTIMATE GOAL FOR THIS YEAR:	NOTES:

TODAY'S DATE _____

When you come to the end of your rope, tie a knot and hang on.
Franklin D. Roosevelt

MY GOALS FOR TODAY:	CALLS AND CONTACTS TO MAKE TODAY:
1.	
2.	
3.	
4.	
5.	SCHEDULED EVENTS AND REMINDERS:
*	
*	
*	
*	
FOR SUPPER TONIGHT WE'LL HAVE:	
MY GOALS FOR THIS WEEK:	MY GOALS FOR THIS MONTH:

TODAY'S DATE _____

Concern should drive us into action and not into a depression.

Karen Horney

MY GOALS FOR TODAY:	CALLS AND CONTACTS TO MAKE TODAY:
1.	
2.	
3.	
4.	
5.	SCHEDULED EVENTS AND REMINDERS:
*	
*	
*	
*	
FOR SUPPER TONIGHT WE'LL HAVE:	
MY ULTIMATE GOAL FOR THIS YEAR:	NOTES:

TODAY'S DATE_____

Explore daily the will of God.

Carl Jung

MY GOALS FOR TODAY:	CALLS AND CONTACTS TO MAKE TODAY:
1.	
2.	
3.	
4.	
5.	SCHEDULED EVENTS AND REMINDERS:
*	
*	
*	
*	
FOR SUPPER TONIGHT WE'LL HAVE:	
MY GOALS FOR THIS WEEK:	MY GOALS FOR THIS MONTH:

TODAY'S DATE _____

Problems are messages . . .

Shakti Gawain

MY GOALS FOR TODAY:	CALLS AND CONTACTS TO MAKE TODAY:
1.	
2.	
3.	
4.	
5.	SCHEDULED EVENTS AND REMINDERS:
*	
*	
*	
*	
FOR SUPPER TONIGHT WE'LL HAVE:	
MY ULTIMATE GOAL FOR THIS YEAR:	NOTES:

TODAY'S DATE _____

It's a rare person who wants to hear
what he doesn't want to hear.

Dick Cavette

MY GOALS FOR TODAY:	CALLS AND CONTACTS TO MAKE TODAY:
1.	
2.	
3.	
4.	
5.	SCHEDULED EVENTS AND REMINDERS:
*	
*	
*	
*	
FOR SUPPER TONIGHT WE'LL HAVE:	
MY GOALS FOR THIS WEEK:	MY GOALS FOR THIS MONTH:

TODAY'S DATE _____

I don't know much about being a millionaire,
but I'll bet I'd be darling at it.

Dorothy Parker

MY GOALS FOR TODAY:	CALLS AND CONTACTS TO MAKE TODAY:
1.	
2.	
3.	
4.	
5.	SCHEDULED EVENTS AND REMINDERS:
*	
*	
*	
*	
FOR SUPPER TONIGHT WE'LL HAVE:	
MY ULTIMATE GOAL FOR THIS YEAR:	NOTES:

TODAY'S DATE _____

Let a fool hold his tongue and he will pass for a sage.

Publilius Syrus

MY GOALS FOR TODAY:	CALLS AND CONTACTS TO MAKE TODAY:
1.	
2.	
3.	
4.	
5.	SCHEDULED EVENTS AND REMINDERS:
*	
*	
*	
*	
FOR SUPPER TONIGHT WE'LL HAVE:	
MY GOALS FOR THIS WEEK:	MY GOALS FOR THIS MONTH:

TODAY'S DATE _____

You can observe a lot by watching.

Yogi Berra

MY GOALS FOR TODAY:	CALLS AND CONTACTS TO MAKE TODAY:
1.	
2.	
3.	
4.	
5.	SCHEDULED EVENTS AND REMINDERS:
*	
*	
*	
*	
FOR SUPPER TONIGHT WE'LL HAVE:	
MY ULTIMATE GOAL FOR THIS YEAR:	NOTES:

TODAY'S DATE _____

Only a very exceptionally gifted mind could cope singly with all
the problems which present themselves
in the perfection of a home.

Arnold Bennett

MY GOALS FOR TODAY:	CALLS AND CONTACTS TO MAKE TODAY:
1.	
2.	
3.	
4.	
5.	SCHEDULED EVENTS AND REMINDERS:
*	
*	
*	
*	
FOR SUPPER TONIGHT WE'LL HAVE:	
MY GOALS FOR THIS WEEK:	MY GOALS FOR THIS MONTH:

TODAY'S DATE _____

To find God is but the beginning of wisdom, because then for all
our lives we have to learn His purpose with us
and to live our lives with Him . . .

H. G. Wells

MY GOALS FOR TODAY:	CALLS AND CONTACTS TO MAKE TODAY:
1.	
2.	
3.	
4.	
5.	SCHEDULED EVENTS AND REMINDERS:
*	
*	
*	
*	
FOR SUPPER TONIGHT WE'LL HAVE:	
MY ULTIMATE GOAL FOR THIS YEAR:	NOTES:

TODAY'S DATE _____

Silence is the source of strength.

Lao Tzu

MY GOALS FOR TODAY:	CALLS AND CONTACTS TO MAKE TODAY:
1.	
2.	
3.	
4.	
5.	SCHEDULED EVENTS AND REMINDERS:
*	
*	
*	
*	
FOR SUPPER TONIGHT WE'LL HAVE:	
MY GOALS FOR THIS WEEK:	MY GOALS FOR THIS MONTH:

TODAY'S DATE _____

Even wisdom has to yield to self-interest.

Pindar

MY GOALS FOR TODAY:	CALLS AND CONTACTS TO MAKE TODAY:
1.	
2.	
3.	
4.	
5.	SCHEDULED EVENTS AND REMINDERS:
*	
*	
*	
*	
FOR SUPPER TONIGHT WE'LL HAVE:	
MY ULTIMATE GOAL FOR THIS YEAR:	NOTES:

TODAY'S DATE _____

No pessimist ever discovered the secrets of the stars, or sailed to an uncharted land, or opened a new heaven to the human spirit.

Helen Keller

MY GOALS FOR TODAY:	CALLS AND CONTACTS TO MAKE TODAY:
1.	
2.	
3.	
4.	
5.	SCHEDULED EVENTS AND REMINDERS:
*	
*	
*	
*	
FOR SUPPER TONIGHT WE'LL HAVE:	
MY GOALS FOR THIS WEEK:	MY GOALS FOR THIS MONTH:

TODAY'S DATE _____

Though a man be learned if he does not apply his knowledge,
he resembles the blind man, who,
lamp in hand, cannot see the road. . .

Tibetan saying

MY GOALS FOR TODAY:	CALLS AND CONTACTS TO MAKE TODAY:
1.	
2.	
3.	
4.	
5.	SCHEDULED EVENTS AND REMINDERS:
*	
*	
*	
*	
FOR SUPPER TONIGHT WE'LL HAVE:	
MY ULTIMATE GOAL FOR THIS YEAR:	NOTES:

TODAY'S DATE _____

Genius, that power which dazzles mortal eyes,
is oft but perseverance in disguise. . .

Henry Austin

MY GOALS FOR TODAY:	CALLS AND CONTACTS TO MAKE TODAY:
1.	
2.	
3.	
4.	
5.	SCHEDULED EVENTS AND REMINDERS:
*	
*	
*	
*	
FOR SUPPER TONIGHT WE'LL HAVE:	
MY GOALS FOR THIS WEEK:	MY GOALS FOR THIS MONTH:

TODAY'S DATE _____

Your freedom to choose a positive attitude is the treasure God will let no one take from you . . .

Robert Schuller

MY GOALS FOR TODAY:	CALLS AND CONTACTS TO MAKE TODAY:
1.	
2.	
3.	
4.	
5.	SCHEDULED EVENTS AND REMINDERS:
*	
*	
*	
*	
FOR SUPPER TONIGHT WE'LL HAVE:	
MY ULTIMATE GOAL FOR THIS YEAR:	NOTES:

TODAY'S DATE _____

Always tell the truth that way you don't have
to remember what you said.

Mark Twain

MY GOALS FOR TODAY:	CALLS AND CONTACTS TO MAKE TODAY:
1.	
2.	
3.	
4.	
5.	SCHEDULED EVENTS AND REMINDERS:
*	
*	
*	
*	
FOR SUPPER TONIGHT WE'LL HAVE:	
MY GOALS FOR THIS WEEK:	MY GOALS FOR THIS MONTH:

TODAY'S DATE _____

*Great spirits have always encountered violent
opposition from mediocre minds.*

Albert Einstein

MY GOALS FOR TODAY:	CALLS AND CONTACTS TO MAKE TODAY:
1.	
2.	
3.	
4.	
5.	SCHEDULED EVENTS AND REMINDERS:
*	
*	
*	
*	
FOR SUPPER TONIGHT WE'LL HAVE:	
MY ULTIMATE GOAL FOR THIS YEAR:	NOTES:

TODAY'S DATE _____

One sees great things from the valley,
only small things from the peak.

G.K. Chesterton

MY GOALS FOR TODAY:	CALLS AND CONTACTS TO MAKE TODAY:
1.	
2.	
3.	
4.	
5.	SCHEDULED EVENTS AND REMINDERS:
*	
*	
*	
*	
FOR SUPPER TONIGHT WE'LL HAVE:	
MY GOALS FOR THIS WEEK:	MY GOALS FOR THIS MONTH:

TODAY'S DATE _____

Virtue is never left to stand alone.
He who has it will have neighbors.

Confucius

MY GOALS FOR TODAY:	CALLS AND CONTACTS TO MAKE TODAY:
1.	
2.	
3.	
4.	
5.	SCHEDULED EVENTS AND REMINDERS:
*	
*	
*	
*	
FOR SUPPER TONIGHT WE'LL HAVE:	
MY ULTIMATE GOAL FOR THIS YEAR:	NOTES:

MAY

Roses now are in bloom. Stop and smell them right at noon.
Permit mother time to take things slow,
allowing her to just let life flow.
Happy days are just ahead, no more snow there's sun instead.

1	
2	
3	
4	
5	
6	
7	
8	
9	
10	
11	
12	
13	
14	
15	
16	
17	
18	
19	
20	

21	
22	
23	
24	
25	
26	
27	
28	
29	
30	
31	

FUN THINGS TO DO THIS MONTH:

1. Pick or plant some Shasta daisies.
2. President Woodrow Wilson named the second Sunday in May, Mother's Day, in 1914. Give your children an example of how to treat you, by showing them how you remember your own mother with loving gestures.
3. Look up the history of how Memorial Day got started; then hang the stars and stripes.
4. This is a good month to plant the "secret garden" in your Creative Discovery Journal. If you're short on room – three pots, bamboo sticks and morning glories or sweet peas can make a living teepee to hide in.
5. Have a picnic with fried chicken, baked beans, potato salad and lemon-aid. Buy some cheap plastic bats and balls and have an impromptu baseball game in your backyard.
6. Enjoy the smell of fresh cut grass.

MUST DO THIS MONTH

1. I will work on this character trait during May.

_____

2. I will work on these goals this month:

_____

TODAY'S DATE _____

We can be our own best friends or
we can be our own worst enemies. . .

Ralph W. Trine

MY GOALS FOR TODAY:	CALLS AND CONTACTS TO MAKE TODAY:
1.	
2.	
3.	
4.	
5.	SCHEDULED EVENTS AND REMINDERS:
*	
*	
*	
*	
FOR SUPPER TONIGHT WE'LL HAVE:	
MY GOALS FOR THIS WEEK:	MY GOALS FOR THIS MONTH:

TODAY'S DATE _____

Your enthusiasm is not dead;
it merely hides below your cynical practicality. . .

David Seabury

MY GOALS FOR TODAY:	CALLS AND CONTACTS TO MAKE TODAY:
1.	
2.	
3.	
4.	
5.	SCHEDULED EVENTS AND REMINDERS:
*	
*	
*	
*	
FOR SUPPER TONIGHT WE'LL HAVE:	
MY ULTIMATE GOAL FOR THIS YEAR:	NOTES:

TODAY'S DATE _____

It doesn't matter how many people say it cannot be done or how many people have tried it before; it's important to realize that whatever you're doing, it's your first attempt at it.

Wally Amos

MY GOALS FOR TODAY:	CALLS AND CONTACTS TO MAKE TODAY:
1.	
2.	
3.	
4.	
5.	SCHEDULED EVENTS AND REMINDERS:
*	
*	
*	
*	
FOR SUPPER TONIGHT WE'LL HAVE:	
MY GOALS FOR THIS WEEK:	MY GOALS FOR THIS MONTH:

TODAY'S DATE _____

Every spirit builds itself a house, and beyond its house a world,
and beyond its world a heaven.
Know then that world exists for you.

Ralph Waldo Emerson

MY GOALS FOR TODAY:	CALLS AND CONTACTS TO MAKE TODAY:
1.	
2.	
3.	
4.	
5.	SCHEDULED EVENTS AND REMINDERS:
*	
*	
*	
*	
FOR SUPPER TONIGHT WE'LL HAVE:	
MY ULTIMATE GOAL FOR THIS YEAR:	NOTES:

TODAY'S DATE _____

Be a friend to thyself, and others will be so too. . .

Thomas Fuller

MY GOALS FOR TODAY:	CALLS AND CONTACTS TO MAKE TODAY:
1.	
2.	
3.	
4.	
5.	SCHEDULED EVENTS AND REMINDERS:
*	
*	
*	
*	
FOR SUPPER TONIGHT WE'LL HAVE:	
MY GOALS FOR THIS WEEK:	MY GOALS FOR THIS MONTH:

TODAY'S DATE _____

If you can dream it you can do it.

Walt Disney

MY GOALS FOR TODAY:	CALLS AND CONTACTS TO MAKE TODAY:
1.	
2.	
3.	
4.	
5.	SCHEDULED EVENTS AND REMINDERS:
*	
*	
*	
*	
FOR SUPPER TONIGHT WE'LL HAVE:	
MY ULTIMATE GOAL FOR THIS YEAR:	NOTES:

TODAY'S DATE _____

Happiness is a perfume you cannot pour on others
without getting a few drops on yourself. . .

Ralph W. Emerson

MY GOALS FOR TODAY:	CALLS AND CONTACTS TO MAKE TODAY:
1.	
2.	
3.	
4.	
5.	SCHEDULED EVENTS AND REMINDERS:
*	
*	
*	
*	
FOR SUPPER TONIGHT WE'LL HAVE:	
MY GOALS FOR THIS WEEK:	MY GOALS FOR THIS MONTH:

TODAY'S DATE _____

The most compelling dreams are those that
your heart longs for.

Marcia Wieder

MY GOALS FOR TODAY:	CALLS AND CONTACTS TO MAKE TODAY:
1.	
2.	
3.	
4.	
5.	SCHEDULED EVENTS AND REMINDERS:
*	
*	
*	
*	
FOR SUPPER TONIGHT WE'LL HAVE:	
MY ULTIMATE GOAL FOR THIS YEAR:	NOTES:

TODAY'S DATE _____

The Promised Land always lies
on the other side of the wilderness.

Havelock Ellis

MY GOALS FOR TODAY:	CALLS AND CONTACTS TO MAKE TODAY:
1.	
2.	
3.	
4.	
5.	SCHEDULED EVENTS AND REMINDERS:
*	
*	
*	
*	
FOR SUPPER TONIGHT WE'LL HAVE:	
MY GOALS FOR THIS WEEK:	MY GOALS FOR THIS MONTH:

TODAY'S DATE _____

It's a sad day when you find out that it's not accident or time or fortune but just yourself that kept things from you.

Lillian Hellman

MY GOALS FOR TODAY:	CALLS AND CONTACTS TO MAKE TODAY:
1.	
2.	
3.	
4.	
5.	SCHEDULED EVENTS AND REMINDERS:
*	
*	
*	
*	
FOR SUPPER TONIGHT WE'LL HAVE:	
MY ULTIMATE GOAL FOR THIS YEAR:	NOTES:

TODAY'S DATE _____

It is never too late to be what you might have been.

George Eliot

MY GOALS FOR TODAY:	CALLS AND CONTACTS TO MAKE TODAY:
1.	
2.	
3.	
4.	
5.	SCHEDULED EVENTS AND REMINDERS:
*	
*	
*	
*	
FOR SUPPER TONIGHT WE'LL HAVE:	
MY GOALS FOR THIS WEEK:	MY GOALS FOR THIS MONTH:

TODAY'S DATE _____

Where there is a woman, there is magic.

Ntozake Shange

MY GOALS FOR TODAY:	CALLS AND CONTACTS TO MAKE TODAY:
1.	
2.	
3.	
4.	
5.	SCHEDULED EVENTS AND REMINDERS:
*	
*	
*	
*	
FOR SUPPER TONIGHT WE'LL HAVE:	
MY ULTIMATE GOAL FOR THIS YEAR:	NOTES:

TODAY'S DATE _____

The ordinary arts we practice every day at home are of more importance to the soul than their simplicity might suggest.

Thomas Moore

MY GOALS FOR TODAY:	CALLS AND CONTACTS TO MAKE TODAY:
1.	
2.	
3.	
4.	
5.	SCHEDULED EVENTS AND REMINDERS:
*	
*	
*	
*	
FOR SUPPER TONIGHT WE'LL HAVE:	
MY GOALS FOR THIS WEEK:	MY GOALS FOR THIS MONTH:

TODAY'S DATE _____

Thousand upon thousand of human plans
are not equal to one of Heaven's.

Chinese Proverb

MY GOALS FOR TODAY:	CALLS AND CONTACTS TO MAKE TODAY:
1.	
2.	
3.	
4.	
5.	SCHEDULED EVENTS AND REMINDERS:
*	
*	
*	
*	
FOR SUPPER TONIGHT WE'LL HAVE:	
MY ULTIMATE GOAL FOR THIS YEAR:	NOTES:

TODAY'S DATE _____

By nature, I am a very curious person.

Martha Stewart

MY GOALS FOR TODAY:	CALLS AND CONTACTS TO MAKE TODAY:
1.	
2.	
3.	
4.	
5.	SCHEDULED EVENTS AND REMINDERS:
*	
*	
*	
*	
FOR SUPPER TONIGHT WE'LL HAVE:	
MY GOALS FOR THIS WEEK:	MY GOALS FOR THIS MONTH:

TODAY'S DATE _____

You are meant to have an amazing life.

Rhonda Byrne

MY GOALS FOR TODAY:	CALLS AND CONTACTS TO MAKE TODAY:
1.	
2.	
3.	
4.	
5.	SCHEDULED EVENTS AND REMINDERS:
*	
*	
*	
*	
FOR SUPPER TONIGHT WE'LL HAVE:	
MY ULTIMATE GOAL FOR THIS YEAR:	NOTES:

TODAY'S DATE _____

Love is the most powerful and still most unknown
energy in the world.

Pierre Teilhard de Chardin

MY GOALS FOR TODAY:	CALLS AND CONTACTS TO MAKE TODAY:
1.	
2.	
3.	
4.	
5.	SCHEDULED EVENTS AND REMINDERS:
*	
*	
*	
*	
FOR SUPPER TONIGHT WE'LL HAVE:	
MY GOALS FOR THIS WEEK:	MY GOALS FOR THIS MONTH:

TODAY'S DATE _____

Give, and it will be given to you . . . for by your standard of measure it will be measured to you in return.

Jesus

MY GOALS FOR TODAY:	CALLS AND CONTACTS TO MAKE TODAY:
1.	
2.	
3.	
4.	
5.	SCHEDULED EVENTS AND REMINDERS:
*	
*	
*	
*	
FOR SUPPER TONIGHT WE'LL HAVE:	
MY ULTIMATE GOAL FOR THIS YEAR:	NOTES:

TODAY'S DATE _____

When it comes to creating wealth, wealth is a mindset.
It's all about how you think.

David Schirmer

MY GOALS FOR TODAY:	CALLS AND CONTACTS TO MAKE TODAY:
1.	
2.	
3.	
4.	
5.	SCHEDULED EVENTS AND REMINDERS:
*	
*	
*	
*	
FOR SUPPER TONIGHT WE'LL HAVE:	
MY GOALS FOR THIS WEEK:	MY GOALS FOR THIS MONTH:

TODAY'S DATE _____

*How can you ever expect anyone else to enjoy your company
if you don't enjoy your own company?*

James Ray

MY GOALS FOR TODAY:	CALLS AND CONTACTS TO MAKE TODAY:
1.	
2.	
3.	
4.	
5.	SCHEDULED EVENTS AND REMINDERS:
*	
*	
*	
*	
FOR SUPPER TONIGHT WE'LL HAVE:	
MY ULTIMATE GOAL FOR THIS YEAR:	NOTES:

TODAY'S DATE _____

I shut my eyes in order to see.

Paul Gauguin

MY GOALS FOR TODAY:	CALLS AND CONTACTS TO MAKE TODAY:
1.	
2.	
3.	
4.	
5.	SCHEDULED EVENTS AND REMINDERS:
*	
*	
*	
*	
FOR SUPPER TONIGHT WE'LL HAVE:	
MY GOALS FOR THIS WEEK:	MY GOALS FOR THIS MONTH:

TODAY'S DATE _____

Upon the conduct of each depends the fate of all.

Alexander the Great

MY GOALS FOR TODAY:	CALLS AND CONTACTS TO MAKE TODAY:
1.	
2.	
3.	
4.	
5.	SCHEDULED EVENTS AND REMINDERS:
*	
*	
*	
*	
FOR SUPPER TONIGHT WE'LL HAVE:	
MY ULTIMATE GOAL FOR THIS YEAR:	NOTES:

JUNE

Enjoy your summer out of doors. Build a fire and make some s'mores.
Lightning bugs are on the wing.
Listen to the crickets sing.

1	
2	
3	
4	
5	
6	
7	
8	
9	
10	
11	
12	
13	
14	
15	
16	
17	
18	
19	
20	
21	
22	

23	
24	
25	
26	
27	
28	
29	
30	

FUN THINGS TO DO THIS MONTH:

1. Lie in a hammock with a child or alone, and look up at the clouds. What shapes can you find? A boat? A whale? A president?
2. 1972 was the first year Father's Day was officially celebrated. Acknowledge Dad on Father's Day, by telling him thanks for all he does.
3. June 21st is the Summer Solstice – the longest day of the year. Celebrate summer by camping out. Build a fire and have hot dogs for supper. Make s'mores for dessert. When everyone is finished eating and the embers of the fire are glowing hot, tell some ghost stories. Maybe you could just tell a few stories from your past. Children love hearing about your childhood.
4. Pick some raspberries or blackberries and make some jam. It's easier than you think.
5. When I was a child a favorite pastime was to walk in mud puddles after a summer rain. Allow your children to get dirty. Join in. It's lots of fun.
6. Catch some lightning bugs. Put them in a Mason jar. Punch a few holes in the lid to give them air. Put some grass in the bottom to make them comfortable. Let them out before going to bed.

MUST DO THIS MONTH

1. I will work on this character trait during June.

_____

2. I will work on these goals this month:

_____

TODAY'S DATE _____

Understanding is the elixir of life.

Mike Dooley

MY GOALS FOR TODAY:	CALLS AND CONTACTS TO MAKE TODAY:
1.	
2.	
3.	
4.	
5.	SCHEDULED EVENTS AND REMINDERS:
*	
*	
*	
*	
FOR SUPPER TONIGHT WE'LL HAVE:	
MY GOALS FOR THIS WEEK:	MY GOALS FOR THIS MONTH:

TODAY'S DATE _____

Power comes from inner strength.

Neale Donald Walsch

MY GOALS FOR TODAY:	CALLS AND CONTACTS TO MAKE TODAY:
1.	
2.	
3.	
4.	
5.	SCHEDULED EVENTS AND REMINDERS:
*	
*	
*	
*	
FOR SUPPER TONIGHT WE'LL HAVE:	
MY ULTIMATE GOAL FOR THIS YEAR:	NOTES:

TODAY'S DATE _____

The best way to predict the future is to create it.

Peter F. Drucker

MY GOALS FOR TODAY:	CALLS AND CONTACTS TO MAKE TODAY:
1.	
2.	
3.	
4.	
5.	SCHEDULED EVENTS AND REMINDERS:
*	
*	
*	
*	
FOR SUPPER TONIGHT WE'LL HAVE:	
MY GOALS FOR THIS WEEK:	MY GOALS FOR THIS MONTH:

TODAY'S DATE _____

Life changes but memories live on forever.
Sarah Ban Breathnach

MY GOALS FOR TODAY:	CALLS AND CONTACTS TO MAKE TODAY:
1.	
2.	
3.	
4.	
5.	SCHEDULED EVENTS AND REMINDERS:
*	
*	
*	
*	
FOR SUPPER TONIGHT WE'LL HAVE:	
MY ULTIMATE GOAL FOR THIS YEAR:	NOTES:

TODAY'S DATE _____

Life lived for tomorrow will always be
just a day away from being realized.

Leo Buscaglia

MY GOALS FOR TODAY:	CALLS AND CONTACTS TO MAKE TODAY:
1.	
2.	
3.	
4.	
5.	SCHEDULED EVENTS AND REMINDERS:
*	
*	
*	
*	
FOR SUPPER TONIGHT WE'LL HAVE:	
MY GOALS FOR THIS WEEK:	MY GOALS FOR THIS MONTH:

TODAY'S DATE _____

Work without faith is like an attempt
to reach the bottom of a bottomless pit. . .

Mohandas Gandhi

MY GOALS FOR TODAY:	CALLS AND CONTACTS TO MAKE TODAY:
1.	
2.	
3.	
4.	
5.	SCHEDULED EVENTS AND REMINDERS:
*	
*	
*	
*	
FOR SUPPER TONIGHT WE'LL HAVE:	
MY ULTIMATE GOAL FOR THIS YEAR:	NOTES:

TODAY'S DATE _____

The question is not really whether or not you go on,
but rather how are you going to enjoy it?

Robert Churman

MY GOALS FOR TODAY:	CALLS AND CONTACTS TO MAKE TODAY:
1.	
2.	
3.	
4.	
5.	SCHEDULED EVENTS AND REMINDERS:
*	
*	
*	
*	
FOR SUPPER TONIGHT WE'LL HAVE:	
MY GOALS FOR THIS WEEK:	MY GOALS FOR THIS MONTH:

TODAY'S DATE _____

Decide who you are — who you want to be — and then do everything in your power to be that.

Neal Donald Walsh

MY GOALS FOR TODAY:	CALLS AND CONTACTS TO MAKE TODAY:
1.	
2.	
3.	
4.	
5.	SCHEDULED EVENTS AND REMINDERS:
*	
*	
*	
*	
FOR SUPPER TONIGHT WE'LL HAVE:	
MY ULTIMATE GOAL FOR THIS YEAR:	NOTES:

TODAY'S DATE _____

*We all come with a built-in basic program. It's called
"self-healing." You get a wound, it grows back together.*

Dr. Ben Johnson

MY GOALS FOR TODAY:	CALLS AND CONTACTS TO MAKE TODAY:
1.	
2.	
3.	
4.	
5.	SCHEDULED EVENTS AND REMINDERS:
*	
*	
*	
*	
FOR SUPPER TONIGHT WE'LL HAVE:	
MY GOALS FOR THIS WEEK:	MY GOALS FOR THIS MONTH:

TODAY'S DATE _____

Some people . . . are born with an ability to empathize. For
others it takes a bit of time to develop the appropriate attitude.

Martha Stewart

MY GOALS FOR TODAY:	CALLS AND CONTACTS TO MAKE TODAY:
1.	
2.	
3.	
4.	
5.	SCHEDULED EVENTS AND REMINDERS:
*	
*	
*	
*	
FOR SUPPER TONIGHT WE'LL HAVE:	
MY ULTIMATE GOAL FOR THIS YEAR:	NOTES:

TODAY'S DATE _____

*No one is kept in poverty by a shortness in the supply of riches;
there is more than enough for all.*

Wallace Wattles

MY GOALS FOR TODAY:	CALLS AND CONTACTS TO MAKE TODAY:
1.	
2.	
3.	
4.	
5.	SCHEDULED EVENTS AND REMINDERS:
*	
*	
*	
*	
FOR SUPPER TONIGHT WE'LL HAVE:	
MY GOALS FOR THIS WEEK:	MY GOALS FOR THIS MONTH:

TODAY'S DATE _____

Every person was designed with the ability to serve, with a potential capacity to serve in an unlimited fashion.

J. Jones

MY GOALS FOR TODAY:	CALLS AND CONTACTS TO MAKE TODAY:
1.	
2.	
3.	
4.	
5.	SCHEDULED EVENTS AND REMINDERS:
*	
*	
*	
*	
FOR SUPPER TONIGHT WE'LL HAVE:	
MY ULTIMATE GOAL FOR THIS YEAR:	NOTES:

TODAY'S DATE _____

A happy life consists in tranquility of mind.

Cicero

MY GOALS FOR TODAY:	CALLS AND CONTACTS TO MAKE TODAY:
1.	
2.	
3.	
4.	
5.	SCHEDULED EVENTS AND REMINDERS:
*	
*	
*	
*	
FOR SUPPER TONIGHT WE'LL HAVE:	
MY GOALS FOR THIS WEEK:	MY GOALS FOR THIS MONTH:

TODAY'S DATE _____

Whatever you'd like to know, you already know. Be still.

Mike Dooley

MY GOALS FOR TODAY:	CALLS AND CONTACTS TO MAKE TODAY:
1.	
2.	
3.	
4.	
5.	SCHEDULED EVENTS AND REMINDERS:
*	
*	
*	
*	
FOR SUPPER TONIGHT WE'LL HAVE:	
MY ULTIMATE GOAL FOR THIS YEAR:	NOTES:

TODAY'S DATE _____

When you're born of the Spirit you're made so brand new and all the time you wasted is given back to you.

Michael Bernard Beckwith

MY GOALS FOR TODAY:	CALLS AND CONTACTS TO MAKE TODAY:
1.	
2.	
3.	
4.	
5.	SCHEDULED EVENTS AND REMINDERS:
*	
*	
*	
*	
FOR SUPPER TONIGHT WE'LL HAVE:	
MY GOALS FOR THIS WEEK:	MY GOALS FOR THIS MONTH:

TODAY'S DATE _____

*I was seldom able to see an opportunity until
it had ceased to be one.*

Mark Twain

MY GOALS FOR TODAY:	CALLS AND CONTACTS TO MAKE TODAY:
1.	
2.	
3.	
4.	
5.	SCHEDULED EVENTS AND REMINDERS:
*	
*	
*	
*	
FOR SUPPER TONIGHT WE'LL HAVE:	
MY ULTIMATE GOAL FOR THIS YEAR:	NOTES:

TODAY'S DATE _____

I am certain of nothing but the holiness of the heart's affections
and the truth of the imagination.

John Keats

MY GOALS FOR TODAY:	CALLS AND CONTACTS TO MAKE TODAY:
1.	
2.	
3.	
4.	
5.	SCHEDULED EVENTS AND REMINDERS:
*	
*	
*	
*	
FOR SUPPER TONIGHT WE'LL HAVE:	
MY GOALS FOR THIS WEEK:	MY GOALS FOR THIS MONTH:

TODAY'S DATE _____

If you can dream it, then you can achieve it. You get all you want
in life if you help enough people get what they want.

Zig Ziglar

MY GOALS FOR TODAY:	CALLS AND CONTACTS TO MAKE TODAY:
1.	
2.	
3.	
4.	
5.	SCHEDULED EVENTS AND REMINDERS:
*	
*	
*	
*	
FOR SUPPER TONIGHT WE'LL HAVE:	
MY ULTIMATE GOAL FOR THIS YEAR:	NOTES:

TODAY'S DATE _____

Today's impossibilities are tomorrow's miracles.

Robert Schuller

MY GOALS FOR TODAY:	CALLS AND CONTACTS TO MAKE TODAY:
1.	
2.	
3.	
4.	
5.	SCHEDULED EVENTS AND REMINDERS:
*	
*	
*	
*	
FOR SUPPER TONIGHT WE'LL HAVE:	
MY GOALS FOR THIS WEEK:	MY GOALS FOR THIS MONTH:

TODAY'S DATE _____

Attitude is a little thing that makes a big difference.

Winston Churchill

MY GOALS FOR TODAY:	CALLS AND CONTACTS TO MAKE TODAY:
1.	
2.	
3.	
4.	
5.	SCHEDULED EVENTS AND REMINDERS:
*	
*	
*	
*	
FOR SUPPER TONIGHT WE'LL HAVE:	
MY ULTIMATE GOAL FOR THIS YEAR:	NOTES:

TODAY'S DATE _____

Only a life lived for others is worth living.

Albert Einstein

MY GOALS FOR TODAY:	CALLS AND CONTACTS TO MAKE TODAY:
1.	
2.	
3.	
4.	
5.	SCHEDULED EVENTS AND REMINDERS:
*	
*	
*	
*	
FOR SUPPER TONIGHT WE'LL HAVE:	
MY GOALS FOR THIS WEEK:	MY GOALS FOR THIS MONTH:

TODAY'S DATE _____

Great works are performed not by strength but by perseverance
Samuel Johnson

MY GOALS FOR TODAY:	CALLS AND CONTACTS TO MAKE TODAY:
1.	
2.	
3.	
4.	
5.	SCHEDULED EVENTS AND REMINDERS:
*	
*	
*	
*	
FOR SUPPER TONIGHT WE'LL HAVE:	
MY ULTIMATE GOAL FOR THIS YEAR:	NOTES:

JULY

Hot fun – in the sun!
Cooling water is a blast. Go swimming now while summer lasts.
Celebrate the 4th of July – by watching explosions in the sky.
Simple pleasures are the key. Enjoy the sun and honeybees.

1	
2	
3	
4	
5	
6	
7	
8	
9	
10	
11	
12	
13	
14	
15	
16	
17	
18	
19	
20	
21	

22	
23	
24	
25	
26	
27	
28	
29	
30	
31	

FUN THINGS TO DO THIS MONTH:

1. Get together with friends and/or family and visit a beach. Have a contest to see who can make the best sandcastle. Study some real medieval ones before you leave to give you some ideas. Make tall steeples buy getting sand really wet and letting it slide off your fingers.
2. Read the book, *Fireworks, Picnics, and Flags*, by James Cross Giblin.
3. Make "real" lemon-aid by squeezing the juice of four lemons into a gallon pitcher. Add 2 cups of sugar, fill with water and stir.
4. Get out the red tablecloth you bought in February. Pair it with some blue and white, checkered, place mats. Make a centerpiece of daisies and mini flags on wooden sticks.
5. Put cherries into an ice cube tray and fill with water. Freeze. Any drink is more appealing with cherry ice cubes floating in it. Or fill ice cube trays with fruit juice; when almost frozen insert toothpicks and make some quick homemade popsicles.

MUST DO THIS MONTH

1. I will work on this character trait during July.

   _____

2. I will work on these goals this month:

   _____

TODAY'S DATE_____

A journey is like a marriage. The certain way to be wrong is to think you control it.

John Steinbeck

MY GOALS FOR TODAY:	CALLS AND CONTACTS TO MAKE TODAY:
1.	
2.	
3.	
4.	
5.	SCHEDULED EVENTS AND REMINDERS:
*	
*	
*	
*	
FOR SUPPER TONIGHT WE'LL HAVE:	
MY GOALS FOR THIS WEEK:	MY GOALS FOR THIS MONTH:

TODAY'S DATE _____

Great things are not done by impulse,
but by a series of small things brought together.

Vincent Van Gogh

MY GOALS FOR TODAY:	CALLS AND CONTACTS TO MAKE TODAY:
1.	
2.	
3.	
4.	
5.	SCHEDULED EVENTS AND REMINDERS:
*	
*	
*	
*	
FOR SUPPER TONIGHT WE'LL HAVE:	
MY ULTIMATE GOAL FOR THIS YEAR:	NOTES:

TODAY'S DATE _____

A woman is the only thing I am afraid of
that I know will not hurt me.

Abraham Lincoln

MY GOALS FOR TODAY:	CALLS AND CONTACTS TO MAKE TODAY:
1.	
2.	
3.	
4.	
5.	SCHEDULED EVENTS AND REMINDERS:
*	
*	
*	
*	
FOR SUPPER TONIGHT WE'LL HAVE:	
MY GOALS FOR THIS WEEK:	MY GOALS FOR THIS MONTH:

TODAY'S DATE _____

He who is not courageous enough to take risks
will accomplish nothing in life.

Muhammad Ali

MY GOALS FOR TODAY:	CALLS AND CONTACTS TO MAKE TODAY:
1.	
2.	
3.	
4.	
5.	SCHEDULED EVENTS AND REMINDERS:
*	
*	
*	
*	
FOR SUPPER TONIGHT WE'LL HAVE:	
MY ULTIMATE GOAL FOR THIS YEAR:	NOTES:

TODAY'S DATE _____

Better three hours too soon than a minute too late.

William Shakespeare

MY GOALS FOR TODAY:	CALLS AND CONTACTS TO MAKE TODAY:
1.	
2.	
3.	
4.	
5.	SCHEDULED EVENTS AND REMINDERS:
*	
*	
*	
*	
FOR SUPPER TONIGHT WE'LL HAVE:	
MY GOALS FOR THIS WEEK:	MY GOALS FOR THIS MONTH:

TODAY'S DATE _____

All great change in America begins at the dinner table.

Ronald Regan

MY GOALS FOR TODAY:	CALLS AND CONTACTS TO MAKE TODAY:
1.	
2.	
3.	
4.	
5.	SCHEDULED EVENTS AND REMINDERS:
*	
*	
*	
*	
FOR SUPPER TONIGHT WE'LL HAVE:	
MY ULTIMATE GOAL FOR THIS YEAR:	NOTES:

TODAY'S DATE _____

Each one of them is Jesus in disguise.

Mother Teresa

MY GOALS FOR TODAY:	CALLS AND CONTACTS TO MAKE TODAY:
1.	
2.	
3.	
4.	
5.	SCHEDULED EVENTS AND REMINDERS:
*	
*	
*	
*	
FOR SUPPER TONIGHT WE'LL HAVE:	
MY GOALS FOR THIS WEEK:	MY GOALS FOR THIS MONTH:

TODAY'S DATE _____

Be polite to all but intimate with a few.

Thomas Jefferson

MY GOALS FOR TODAY:	CALLS AND CONTACTS TO MAKE TODAY:
1.	
2.	
3.	
4.	
5.	SCHEDULED EVENTS AND REMINDERS:
*	
*	
*	
*	
FOR SUPPER TONIGHT WE'LL HAVE:	
MY ULTIMATE GOAL FOR THIS YEAR:	NOTES:

TODAY'S DATE _____

There are only two ways to live your life.
One is as though nothing is a miracle.
The other is as though everything is a miracle.

Albert Einstein

MY GOALS FOR TODAY:	CALLS AND CONTACTS TO MAKE TODAY:
1.	
2.	
3.	
4.	
5.	SCHEDULED EVENTS AND REMINDERS:
*	
*	
*	
*	
FOR SUPPER TONIGHT WE'LL HAVE:	
MY GOALS FOR THIS WEEK:	MY GOALS FOR THIS MONTH:

TODAY'S DATE _____

Quality should be placed at the top of your list of priorities,
and it should remain there. Quality is something you
should strive for in every decision, every day.

Martha Stewart

MY GOALS FOR TODAY:	CALLS AND CONTACTS TO MAKE TODAY:
1.	
2.	
3.	
4.	
5.	SCHEDULED EVENTS AND REMINDERS:
*	
*	
*	
*	
FOR SUPPER TONIGHT WE'LL HAVE:	
MY ULTIMATE GOAL FOR THIS YEAR:	NOTES:

TODAY'S DATE _____

Any fool can criticize, condemn, and complain.
And most fools do.

Benjamin Franklin

MY GOALS FOR TODAY:	CALLS AND CONTACTS TO MAKE TODAY:
1.	
2.	
3.	
4.	
5.	SCHEDULED EVENTS AND REMINDERS:
*	
*	
*	
*	
FOR SUPPER TONIGHT WE'LL HAVE:	
MY GOALS FOR THIS WEEK:	MY GOALS FOR THIS MONTH:

TODAY'S DATE _____

A man's character may be learned from the adjectives
which he habitually uses in conversation.

Mark Twain

MY GOALS FOR TODAY:	CALLS AND CONTACTS TO MAKE TODAY:
1.	
2.	
3.	
4.	
5.	SCHEDULED EVENTS AND REMINDERS:
*	
*	
*	
*	
FOR SUPPER TONIGHT WE'LL HAVE:	
MY ULTIMATE GOAL FOR THIS YEAR:	NOTES:

TODAY'S DATE _____

A real decision is measured by the fact that you've taken a new action. If there's no action, you haven't truly decided.

Tony Robbins

MY GOALS FOR TODAY:	CALLS AND CONTACTS TO MAKE TODAY:
1.	
2.	
3.	
4.	
5.	SCHEDULED EVENTS AND REMINDERS:
*	
*	
*	
*	
FOR SUPPER TONIGHT WE'LL HAVE:	
MY GOALS FOR THIS WEEK:	MY GOALS FOR THIS MONTH:

TODAY'S DATE _____

Many people who order their lives rightly in all other ways are kept in poverty by their lack of gratitude.

Wallace Wattles

MY GOALS FOR TODAY:	CALLS AND CONTACTS TO MAKE TODAY:
1.	
2.	
3.	
4.	
5.	SCHEDULED EVENTS AND REMINDERS:
*	
*	
*	
*	
FOR SUPPER TONIGHT WE'LL HAVE:	
MY ULTIMATE GOAL FOR THIS YEAR:	NOTES:

TODAY'S DATE _____

*Sometimes one creates a dynamic impression by saying something,
and sometimes one creates as significant
impression by remaining silent.*

Dalai Lama

MY GOALS FOR TODAY:	CALLS AND CONTACTS TO MAKE TODAY:
1.	
2.	
3.	
4.	
5.	SCHEDULED EVENTS AND REMINDERS:
*	
*	
*	
*	
FOR SUPPER TONIGHT WE'LL HAVE:	
MY GOALS FOR THIS WEEK:	MY GOALS FOR THIS MONTH:

TODAY'S DATE _____

I pray that you will follow your star and generate
the miracles that will lead you, and all of us,
on the path of creating heaven on earth.

Kathleen McGowan

MY GOALS FOR TODAY:	CALLS AND CONTACTS TO MAKE TODAY:
1.	
2.	
3.	
4.	
5.	SCHEDULED EVENTS AND REMINDERS:
*	
*	
*	
*	
FOR SUPPER TONIGHT WE'LL HAVE:	
MY ULTIMATE GOAL FOR THIS YEAR:	NOTES:

TODAY'S DATE _____

God's gifts put man's best dreams to shame.

Elizabeth Barrett Browning

MY GOALS FOR TODAY:	CALLS AND CONTACTS TO MAKE TODAY:
1.	
2.	
3.	
4.	
5.	SCHEDULED EVENTS AND REMINDERS:
*	
*	
*	
*	
FOR SUPPER TONIGHT WE'LL HAVE:	
MY GOALS FOR THIS WEEK:	MY GOALS FOR THIS MONTH:

TODAY'S DATE _____

Things come suitable to their time.

Enid Bagnold

MY GOALS FOR TODAY:	CALLS AND CONTACTS TO MAKE TODAY:
1.	
2.	
3.	
4.	
5.	SCHEDULED EVENTS AND REMINDERS:
*	
*	
*	
*	
FOR SUPPER TONIGHT WE'LL HAVE:	
MY ULTIMATE GOAL FOR THIS YEAR:	NOTES:

TODAY'S DATE _____

Well-being is not a state of mind or even of body.
It is a state of grace.

Sally Brampton

MY GOALS FOR TODAY:	CALLS AND CONTACTS TO MAKE TODAY:
1.	
2.	
3.	
4.	
5.	SCHEDULED EVENTS AND REMINDERS:
*	
*	
*	
*	
FOR SUPPER TONIGHT WE'LL HAVE:	
MY GOALS FOR THIS WEEK:	MY GOALS FOR THIS MONTH:

TODAY'S DATE _____

Connecting with family is one of the most deeply
restorative acts of self —love we can choose.

Sonia Choquette

MY GOALS FOR TODAY:	CALLS AND CONTACTS TO MAKE TODAY:
1.	
2.	
3.	
4.	
5.	SCHEDULED EVENTS AND REMINDERS:
*	
*	
*	
*	
FOR SUPPER TONIGHT WE'LL HAVE:	
MY ULTIMATE GOAL FOR THIS YEAR:	NOTES:

TODAY'S DATE _____

A #2 pencil and a dream can take you anywhere.

Joyce A. Myers

MY GOALS FOR TODAY:	CALLS AND CONTACTS TO MAKE TODAY:
1.	
2.	
3.	
4.	
5.	SCHEDULED EVENTS AND REMINDERS:
*	
*	
*	
*	
FOR SUPPER TONIGHT WE'LL HAVE:	
MY GOALS FOR THIS WEEK:	MY GOALS FOR THIS MONTH:

TODAY'S DATE _____

Believe you can and you're halfway there.

Theodore Roosevelt

MY GOALS FOR TODAY:	CALLS AND CONTACTS TO MAKE TODAY:
1.	
2.	
3.	
4.	
5.	SCHEDULED EVENTS AND REMINDERS:
*	
*	
*	
*	
FOR SUPPER TONIGHT WE'LL HAVE:	
MY ULTIMATE GOAL FOR THIS YEAR:	NOTES:

☼AUGUST☼

Sultry summer days – if Mother Nature has her ways.
Family reunions bring loved ones home.
Everyone enjoys eating an ice cream cone.
Grasshoppers and bales of hay – we begin
to think summer is here to stay.

1	
2	
3	
4	
5	
6	
7	
8	
9	
10	
11	
12	
13	
14	
15	
16	
17	
18	
19	
20	

21	
22	
23	
24	
25	
26	
27	
28	
29	
30	
31	

FUN THINGS TO DO THIS MONTH:

1. Marvel at the power of nature during a storm. Teach children how the earth benefits from lightning. Did you know that each year lightning produces around 250,000 tons of nitrate fertilizer? It also produces negative ions which can improve your mood.
2. Blow some bubbles with your kids and relish in the rainbows and their delicacy.
3. Sit and watch the sun go down. Teach children what makes the sky red.
4. Make a taco buffet for supper. Let children help. Brown ground beef. Season it with salt and a few red pepper flakes. Chop an onion. Tear up some lettuce. Grate some cheese. Pull the leaves off a few stalks of cilantro. Cut 2 avocados in half, pit, scoop out contents, and mash. Cut up some tomatoes. Supper is served!

MUST DO THIS MONTH

1. I will work on this character trait during August.

   _____

2. I will work on these goals this month.

   _____

TODAY'S DATE _____

Give light and people will find the way.

Ella Baker

MY GOALS FOR TODAY:	CALLS AND CONTACTS TO MAKE TODAY:
1.	
2.	
3.	
4.	
5.	SCHEDULED EVENTS AND REMINDERS:
*	
*	
*	
*	
FOR SUPPER TONIGHT WE'LL HAVE:	
MY GOALS FOR THIS WEEK:	MY GOALS FOR THIS MONTH:

TODAY'S DATE _____

Knowledge comes, but wisdom lingers.

Alfred Lord Tennyson

MY GOALS FOR TODAY:	CALLS AND CONTACTS TO MAKE TODAY:
1.	
2.	
3.	
4.	
5.	SCHEDULED EVENTS AND REMINDERS:
*	
*	
*	
*	
FOR SUPPER TONIGHT WE'LL HAVE:	
MY ULTIMATE GOAL FOR THIS YEAR:	NOTES:

TODAY'S DATE _____

No bird soars too high if he soars with his own wings.

William Blake

MY GOALS FOR TODAY:	CALLS AND CONTACTS TO MAKE TODAY:
1.	
2.	
3.	
4.	
5.	SCHEDULED EVENTS AND REMINDERS:
*	
*	
*	
*	
FOR SUPPER TONIGHT WE'LL HAVE:	
MY GOALS FOR THIS WEEK:	MY GOALS FOR THIS MONTH:

TODAY'S DATE _____

Faith is a passionate intuition.

William Wordsworth

MY GOALS FOR TODAY:	CALLS AND CONTACTS TO MAKE TODAY:
1.	
2.	
3.	
4.	
5.	SCHEDULED EVENTS AND REMINDERS:
*	
*	
*	
*	
FOR SUPPER TONIGHT WE'LL HAVE:	
MY ULTIMATE GOAL FOR THIS YEAR:	NOTES:

TODAY'S DATE _____

Better to be without logic than without feeling.

Charlotte Bronte

MY GOALS FOR TODAY:	CALLS AND CONTACTS TO MAKE TODAY:
1.	
2.	
3.	
4.	
5.	SCHEDULED EVENTS AND REMINDERS:
*	
*	
*	
*	
FOR SUPPER TONIGHT WE'LL HAVE:	
MY GOALS FOR THIS WEEK:	MY GOALS FOR THIS MONTH:

TODAY'S DATE _____

It is the loving, not the loved, woman who feels loveable.
                                                Jessamyn West

MY GOALS FOR TODAY:	CALLS AND CONTACTS TO MAKE TODAY:
1.	
2.	
3.	
4.	
5.	SCHEDULED EVENTS AND REMINDERS:
*	
*	
*	
*	
FOR SUPPER TONIGHT WE'LL HAVE:	
MY ULTIMATE GOAL FOR THIS YEAR:	NOTES:

TODAY'S DATE _____

There are homes you run from, and homes you run to.
Laura Cunningham

MY GOALS FOR TODAY:	CALLS AND CONTACTS TO MAKE TODAY:
1.	
2.	
3.	
4.	
5.	SCHEDULED EVENTS AND REMINDERS:
*	
*	
*	
*	
FOR SUPPER TONIGHT WE'LL HAVE:	
MY GOALS FOR THIS WEEK:	MY GOALS FOR THIS MONTH:

TODAY'S DATE _____

The unendurable is the beginning of the curve to joy.

Djuna Barnes

MY GOALS FOR TODAY:	CALLS AND CONTACTS TO MAKE TODAY:
1.	
2.	
3.	
4.	
5.	SCHEDULED EVENTS AND REMINDERS:
*	
*	
*	
*	
FOR SUPPER TONIGHT WE'LL HAVE:	
MY ULTIMATE GOAL FOR THIS YEAR:	NOTES:

TODAY'S DATE _____

And last, but far from least, remember to make it beautiful.
Martha Stewart

MY GOALS FOR TODAY:	CALLS AND CONTACTS TO MAKE TODAY:
1.	
2.	
3.	
4.	
5.	SCHEDULED EVENTS AND REMINDERS:
*	
*	
*	
*	
FOR SUPPER TONIGHT WE'LL HAVE:	
MY GOALS FOR THIS WEEK:	MY GOALS FOR THIS MONTH:

TODAY'S DATE _____

If you desire faith, then you have faith enough.

Elizabeth Barrett Browning

MY GOALS FOR TODAY:	CALLS AND CONTACTS TO MAKE TODAY:
1.	
2.	
3.	
4.	
5.	SCHEDULED EVENTS AND REMINDERS:
*	
*	
*	
*	
FOR SUPPER TONIGHT WE'LL HAVE:	
MY ULTIMATE GOAL FOR THIS YEAR:	NOTES:

TODAY'S DATE _____

God's voice speaks to me all through the day.

A Course in Miracles

MY GOALS FOR TODAY:	CALLS AND CONTACTS TO MAKE TODAY:
1.	
2.	
3.	
4.	
5.	SCHEDULED EVENTS AND REMINDERS:
*	
*	
*	
*	
FOR SUPPER TONIGHT WE'LL HAVE:	
MY GOALS FOR THIS WEEK:	MY GOALS FOR THIS MONTH:

TODAY'S DATE _____

Joy is not in things, it is in us.

Charles Wagner

MY GOALS FOR TODAY:	CALLS AND CONTACTS TO MAKE TODAY:
1.	
2.	
3.	
4.	
5.	SCHEDULED EVENTS AND REMINDERS:
*	
*	
*	
*	
FOR SUPPER TONIGHT WE'LL HAVE:	
MY ULTIMATE GOAL FOR THIS YEAR:	NOTES:

TODAY'S DATE _____

It is a capital mistake to theorize before one has data.

Author Conan Doyle

MY GOALS FOR TODAY:	CALLS AND CONTACTS TO MAKE TODAY:
1.	
2.	
3.	
4.	
5.	SCHEDULED EVENTS AND REMINDERS:
*	
*	
*	
*	
FOR SUPPER TONIGHT WE'LL HAVE:	
MY GOALS FOR THIS WEEK:	MY GOALS FOR THIS MONTH:

TODAY'S DATE _____

Act as if what you do makes a difference. It does.

William James

MY GOALS FOR TODAY:	CALLS AND CONTACTS TO MAKE TODAY:
1.	
2.	
3.	
4.	
5.	SCHEDULED EVENTS AND REMINDERS:
*	
*	
*	
*	
FOR SUPPER TONIGHT WE'LL HAVE:	
MY ULTIMATE GOAL FOR THIS YEAR:	NOTES:

TODAY'S DATE _____

Always desire to learn something useful.

Sophocles

MY GOALS FOR TODAY:	CALLS AND CONTACTS TO MAKE TODAY:
1.	
2.	
3.	
4.	
5.	SCHEDULED EVENTS AND REMINDERS:
*	
*	
*	
*	
FOR SUPPER TONIGHT WE'LL HAVE:	
MY GOALS FOR THIS WEEK:	MY GOALS FOR THIS MONTH:

TODAY'S DATE _____

Either you run the day or the day runs you.

Jim Rohn

MY GOALS FOR TODAY:	CALLS AND CONTACTS TO MAKE TODAY:
1.	
2.	
3.	
4.	
5.	SCHEDULED EVENTS AND REMINDERS:
*	
*	
*	
*	
FOR SUPPER TONIGHT WE'LL HAVE:	
MY ULTIMATE GOAL FOR THIS YEAR:	NOTES:

TODAY'S DATE _____

*A good head and a good heart are always
a formidable combination.*

Nelson Mandela

MY GOALS FOR TODAY:	CALLS AND CONTACTS TO MAKE TODAY:
1.	
2.	
3.	
4.	
5.	SCHEDULED EVENTS AND REMINDERS:
*	
*	
*	
*	
FOR SUPPER TONIGHT WE'LL HAVE:	
MY GOALS FOR THIS WEEK:	MY GOALS FOR THIS MONTH:

TODAY'S DATE _____

Do not go where the path may lead,
go instead where there is no path and leave a trial.

Ralph Waldo Emerson

MY GOALS FOR TODAY:	CALLS AND CONTACTS TO MAKE TODAY:
1.	
2.	
3.	
4.	
5.	SCHEDULED EVENTS AND REMINDERS:
*	
*	
*	
*	
FOR SUPPER TONIGHT WE'LL HAVE:	
MY ULTIMATE GOAL FOR THIS YEAR:	NOTES:

TODAY'S DATE _____

Discipline is the bridge between goals and accomplishments.
                                                    Jim Rohn

MY GOALS FOR TODAY:	CALLS AND CONTACTS TO MAKE TODAY:
1.	
2.	
3.	
4.	
5.	SCHEDULED EVENTS AND REMINDERS:
*	
*	
*	
*	
FOR SUPPER TONIGHT WE'LL HAVE:	
MY GOALS FOR THIS WEEK:	MY GOALS FOR THIS MONTH:

TODAY'S DATE _____

Always keep an open mind and a compassionate heart.

Phil Jackson

MY GOALS FOR TODAY:	CALLS AND CONTACTS TO MAKE TODAY:
1.	
2.	
3.	
4.	
5.	SCHEDULED EVENTS AND REMINDERS:
*	
*	
*	
*	
FOR SUPPER TONIGHT WE'LL HAVE:	
MY ULTIMATE GOAL FOR THIS YEAR:	NOTES:

TODAY'S DATE _____

Genius is the ability to put into effect what is on your mind.

F. Scott Fitzgerald

MY GOALS FOR TODAY:	CALLS AND CONTACTS TO MAKE TODAY:
1.	
2.	
3.	
4.	
5.	SCHEDULED EVENTS AND REMINDERS:
*	
*	
*	
*	
FOR SUPPER TONIGHT WE'LL HAVE:	
MY GOALS FOR THIS WEEK:	MY GOALS FOR THIS MONTH:

TODAY'S DATE _____

Great work is done by people who are not afraid to be great.

Fernando Flores

MY GOALS FOR TODAY:	CALLS AND CONTACTS TO MAKE TODAY:
1.	
2.	
3.	
4.	
5.	SCHEDULED EVENTS AND REMINDERS:
*	
*	
*	
*	
FOR SUPPER TONIGHT WE'LL HAVE:	
MY GOALS FOR THIS WEEK:	MY GOALS FOR THIS MONTH:

SEPTEMBER

As surely as it began – summer fades like my tan.
Look back on all the things you've done. Simple things were lots of fun.
Like playing in the creek that week – and getting close
to a bluebirds beak.
Now it's time for school to start. Begin it with a happy heart.

1	
2	
3	
4	
5	
6	
7	
8	
9	
10	
11	
12	
13	
14	
15	
16	
17	
18	
19	
20	

21	
22	
23	
24	
25	
26	
27	
28	
29	
30	

FUN THINGS TO DO THIS MONTH:

1. Buy new notebooks, binders, pens, crayons, erasers and things to make everyone excited about starting school.
2. Fall is a good time for reflection. Take a cue from nature. Pare down and re-do if necessary. Are you accomplishing your goals? Stay motivated.
3. Read books together with a theme, then do a related project. An example would be read, *The Swiss Family Robinson*, and build a tree house. It can be a real one outside, or one made of cardboard or blankets – inside.
4. Make a batch of homemade waffles or pancakes for breakfast, and put a smile on everyone's face.
5. Go to a parade on Labor Day. If your kids are ten and under, make sure to bring a blanket, folding chairs, snacks, and drinks. It's fun to give each child their own little brown paper bag of goodies. ☺

MUST DO THIS MONTH

1. Reflect on how and why you are doing things. Ask yourself if there is anything that isn't working or could be working better and make changes for improvement.

   _____

2. I will work on this character trait during September.

   _____

3. I will work on these goals this month:

   _____

TODAY'S DATE _____

I always wanted to be somebody, but now I realize
I should have been more specific.

Lily Tomlin

MY GOALS FOR TODAY:	CALLS AND CONTACTS TO MAKE TODAY:
1.	
2.	
3.	
4.	
5.	SCHEDULED EVENTS AND REMINDERS:
*	
*	
*	
*	
FOR SUPPER TONIGHT WE'LL HAVE:	
MY GOALS FOR THIS WEEK:	MY GOALS FOR THIS MONTH:

TODAY'S DATE _____

If you don't see yourself as a winner,
then you cannot perform as a winner.

Zig Ziglar

MY GOALS FOR TODAY:	CALLS AND CONTACTS TO MAKE TODAY:
1.	
2.	
3.	
4.	
5.	SCHEDULED EVENTS AND REMINDERS:
*	
*	
*	
*	
FOR SUPPER TONIGHT WE'LL HAVE:	
MY ULTIMATE GOAL FOR THIS YEAR:	NOTES:

TODAY'S DATE _____

Peace begins with a smile.

Mother Teresa

MY GOALS FOR TODAY:	CALLS AND CONTACTS TO MAKE TODAY:
1.	
2.	
3.	
4.	
5.	SCHEDULED EVENTS AND REMINDERS:
*	
*	
*	
*	
FOR SUPPER TONIGHT WE'LL HAVE:	
MY GOALS FOR THIS WEEK:	MY GOALS FOR THIS MONTH:

TODAY'S DATE _____

I have never been hurt by what I have not said.

Calvin Coolidge

MY GOALS FOR TODAY:	CALLS AND CONTACTS TO MAKE TODAY:
1.	
2.	
3.	
4.	
5.	SCHEDULED EVENTS AND REMINDERS:
*	
*	
*	
*	
FOR SUPPER TONIGHT WE'LL HAVE:	
MY ULTIMATE GOAL FOR THIS YEAR:	NOTES:

TODAY'S DATE _____

Heroes may not be braver than anyone else.
They're just braver five minutes longer.

Ronald Regan

MY GOALS FOR TODAY:	CALLS AND CONTACTS TO MAKE TODAY:
1.	
2.	
3.	
4.	
5.	SCHEDULED EVENTS AND REMINDERS:
*	
*	
*	
*	
FOR SUPPER TONIGHT WE'LL HAVE:	
MY GOALS FOR THIS WEEK:	MY GOALS FOR THIS MONTH:

TODAY'S DATE _____

Anger is an acid that can do more harm to the vessel in which it
is stored than to anything on which it is poured.

Mark Twain

MY GOALS FOR TODAY:	CALLS AND CONTACTS TO MAKE TODAY:
1.	
2.	
3.	
4.	
5.	SCHEDULED EVENTS AND REMINDERS:
*	
*	
*	
*	
FOR SUPPER TONIGHT WE'LL HAVE:	
MY ULTIMATE GOAL FOR THIS YEAR:	NOTES:

TODAY'S DATE _____

There cannot be a crisis next week. My schedule is already full.
Henry Kissinger

MY GOALS FOR TODAY:	CALLS AND CONTACTS TO MAKE TODAY:
1.	
2.	
3.	
4.	
5.	SCHEDULED EVENTS AND REMINDERS:
*	
*	
*	
*	
FOR SUPPER TONIGHT WE'LL HAVE:	
MY GOALS FOR THIS WEEK:	MY GOALS FOR THIS MONTH:

TODAY'S DATE _____

Who can find a virtuous wife? For her worth is far above rubies.

Proverbs 31:10-12

MY GOALS FOR TODAY:	CALLS AND CONTACTS TO MAKE TODAY:
1.	
2.	
3.	
4.	
5.	SCHEDULED EVENTS AND REMINDERS:
*	
*	
*	
*	
FOR SUPPER TONIGHT WE'LL HAVE:	
MY ULTIMATE GOAL FOR THIS YEAR:	NOTES:

TODAY'S DATE _____

You cannot give to people what they are incapable of receiving.
Agatha Christie

MY GOALS FOR TODAY:	CALLS AND CONTACTS TO MAKE TODAY:
1.	
2.	
3.	
4.	
5.	SCHEDULED EVENTS AND REMINDERS:
*	
*	
*	
*	
FOR SUPPER TONIGHT WE'LL HAVE:	
MY GOALS FOR THIS WEEK:	MY GOALS FOR THIS MONTH:

TODAY'S DATE _____

. . . we need to get up and handle our jobs professionally.

Deniece Schofield

MY GOALS FOR TODAY:	CALLS AND CONTACTS TO MAKE TODAY:
1.	
2.	
3.	
4.	
5.	SCHEDULED EVENTS AND REMINDERS:
*	
*	
*	
*	
FOR SUPPER TONIGHT WE'LL HAVE:	
MY ULTIMATE GOAL FOR THIS YEAR:	NOTES:

TODAY'S DATE _____

Dreams come true. Without that possibility
nature would not incite to have them.

John Updike

MY GOALS FOR TODAY:	CALLS AND CONTACTS TO MAKE TODAY:
1.	
2.	
3.	
4.	
5.	SCHEDULED EVENTS AND REMINDERS:
*	
*	
*	
*	
FOR SUPPER TONIGHT WE'LL HAVE:	
MY GOALS FOR THIS WEEK:	MY GOALS FOR THIS MONTH:

TODAY'S DATE _____

. . . turning our finances over to God's care has often been a route not to poverty but to prosperity.

Julia Cameron

MY GOALS FOR TODAY:	CALLS AND CONTACTS TO MAKE TODAY:
1.	
2.	
3.	
4.	
5.	SCHEDULED EVENTS AND REMINDERS:
*	
*	
*	
*	
FOR SUPPER TONIGHT WE'LL HAVE:	
MY ULTIMATE GOAL FOR THIS YEAR:	NOTES:

TODAY'S DATE _____

If you don't design your own life plan, chances are you'll fall into someone else's plan. And guess what they have planned for you? Not much.

Jim Rohn

MY GOALS FOR TODAY:	CALLS AND CONTACTS TO MAKE TODAY:
1.	
2.	
3.	
4.	
5.	SCHEDULED EVENTS AND REMINDERS:
*	
*	
*	
*	
FOR SUPPER TONIGHT WE'LL HAVE:	
MY GOALS FOR THIS WEEK:	MY GOALS FOR THIS MONTH:

TODAY'S DATE _____

Most of us are going through life with the emergency brake on.
It's time to release the limiting beliefs . . .
that are holding you back.

Jack Canfield

MY GOALS FOR TODAY:	CALLS AND CONTACTS TO MAKE TODAY:
1.	
2.	
3.	
4.	
5.	SCHEDULED EVENTS AND REMINDERS:
*	
*	
*	
*	
FOR SUPPER TONIGHT WE'LL HAVE:	
MY ULTIMATE GOAL FOR THIS YEAR:	NOTES:

TODAY'S DATE _____

Education is not accomplished by putting something into a man;
its purpose is to draw out of man the wisdom
which is latent within him.

Neville

MY GOALS FOR TODAY:	CALLS AND CONTACTS TO MAKE TODAY:
1.	
2.	
3.	
4.	
5.	SCHEDULED EVENTS AND REMINDERS:
*	
*	
*	
*	
FOR SUPPER TONIGHT WE'LL HAVE:	
MY GOALS FOR THIS WEEK:	MY GOALS FOR THIS MONTH:

TODAY'S DATE _____

Yet, even though we are all fairly adaptable . . . we are not born to struggle through life. We are meant to work in ways that suit us, drawing on our natural talents . . . to express ourselves. . .

Marsha Sinetar

MY GOALS FOR TODAY:	CALLS AND CONTACTS TO MAKE TODAY:
1.	
2.	
3.	
4.	
5.	SCHEDULED EVENTS AND REMINDERS:
*	
*	
*	
*	
FOR SUPPER TONIGHT WE'LL HAVE:	
MY ULTIMATE GOAL FOR THIS YEAR:	NOTES:

TODAY'S DATE _____

Nothing changes until you do.

Anonymous

MY GOALS FOR TODAY:	CALLS AND CONTACTS TO MAKE TODAY:
1.	
2.	
3.	
4.	
5.	SCHEDULED EVENTS AND REMINDERS:
*	
*	
*	
*	
FOR SUPPER TONIGHT WE'LL HAVE:	
MY GOALS FOR THIS WEEK:	MY GOALS FOR THIS MONTH:

TODAY'S DATE _____

College isn't the place to go for ideas.

Helen Keller

MY GOALS FOR TODAY:	CALLS AND CONTACTS TO MAKE TODAY:
1.	
2.	
3.	
4.	
5.	SCHEDULED EVENTS AND REMINDERS:
*	
*	
*	
*	
FOR SUPPER TONIGHT WE'LL HAVE:	
MY ULTIMATE GOAL FOR THIS YEAR:	NOTES:

TODAY'S DATE _____

If I am through learning, I am through.

John Wooden

MY GOALS FOR TODAY:	CALLS AND CONTACTS TO MAKE TODAY:
1.	
2.	
3.	
4.	
5.	SCHEDULED EVENTS AND REMINDERS:
*	
*	
*	
*	
FOR SUPPER TONIGHT WE'LL HAVE:	
MY GOALS FOR THIS WEEK:	MY GOALS FOR THIS MONTH:

TODAY'S DATE _____

Don't "should" on yourself.

Sister Patty Campbell

MY GOALS FOR TODAY:	CALLS AND CONTACTS TO MAKE TODAY:
1.	
2.	
3.	
4.	
5.	SCHEDULED EVENTS AND REMINDERS:
*	
*	
*	
*	
FOR SUPPER TONIGHT WE'LL HAVE:	
MY ULTIMATE GOAL FOR THIS YEAR:	NOTES:

TODAY'S DATE _____

I've believed as many as six impossible things before breakfast.
Lewis Carroll

MY GOALS FOR TODAY:	CALLS AND CONTACTS TO MAKE TODAY:
1.	
2.	
3.	
4.	
5.	SCHEDULED EVENTS AND REMINDERS:
*	
*	
*	
*	
FOR SUPPER TONIGHT WE'LL HAVE:	
MY GOALS FOR THIS WEEK:	MY GOALS FOR THIS MONTH:

TODAY'S DATE _____

You will find the key to success under the alarm clock.
Benjamin Franklin

MY GOALS FOR TODAY:	CALLS AND CONTACTS TO MAKE TODAY:
1.	
2.	
3.	
4.	
5.	SCHEDULED EVENTS AND REMINDERS:
*	
*	
*	
*	
FOR SUPPER TONIGHT WE'LL HAVE:	
MY ULTIMATE GOAL FOR THIS YEAR:	NOTES:

❧ OCTOBER ❧

Now's the time for nature's colors – and many more magnificent wonders.
Trees of yellow, red, and gold – gives us peace if truth be told.
Harvest time is right on cue. Squirrels are busy watch what they do.
Each nut is stored with perfect pleasure.
Snow to come we cannot measure.

1	
2	
3	
4	
5	
6	
7	
8	
9	
10	
11	
12	
13	
14	
15	
16	
17	
18	
19	
20	

21	
22	
23	
24	
25	
26	
27	
28	
29	
30	
31	

FUN THINGS TO DO THIS MONTH:

1. Make some monkey bread. Buy (or make your own) frozen bread dough. Let thaw. Cut into ½ inch squares. Dip in equal parts cinnamon and sugar. Put in a buttered bunt pan. Let rise until double. Bake at 350 degrees. For 40 minutes.
2. Start a leaf collection. Glue some pretty leaves onto a plain notebook or folder. Cover with clear contact paper. Fill the inside pages with all different types of leaves. Identify them, and write on each leaf's page what it is and where you found it.
3. Buy a pumpkin. If you have children make sure there is one for each of them. Carve out a special face. There are many different and easy stencils to buy, or make a unique one of your own imagination.
4. Look at all the spectacular colors in nature right now. How many different colors are there on one ear of speckled Indian corn?
5. Have an old-fashioned Halloween party. Play pin the face on the pumpkin and have a scavenger hunt. Have children find things like pinecones, a red leaf, the carcass of a cicada, and a forked stick. Adults love this game too.

MUST DO THIS MONTH

1. I will work on this character trait during October.

   _____

2. I will work on these goals this month:

   _____

TODAY'S DATE _____

If I knew I would've lived this long,
I would've taken better care of myself.

My grandfather, Ray Grunkemeyer

MY GOALS FOR TODAY:	CALLS AND CONTACTS TO MAKE TODAY:
1.	
2.	
3.	
4.	
5.	SCHEDULED EVENTS AND REMINDERS:
*	
*	
*	
*	
FOR SUPPER TONIGHT WE'LL HAVE:	
MY GOALS FOR THIS WEEK:	MY GOALS FOR THIS MONTH:

TODAY'S DATE _____

*Doing more of what doesn't work won't make
it work any better.*

Charles J. Givens

MY GOALS FOR TODAY:	CALLS AND CONTACTS TO MAKE TODAY:
1.	
2.	
3.	
4.	
5.	SCHEDULED EVENTS AND REMINDERS:
*	
*	
*	
*	
FOR SUPPER TONIGHT WE'LL HAVE:	
MY ULTIMATE GOAL FOR THIS YEAR:	NOTES:

TODAY'S DATE _____

Facts do not cease to exist because they are ignored.
Aldous Huxley

MY GOALS FOR TODAY:	CALLS AND CONTACTS TO MAKE TODAY:
1.	
2.	
3.	
4.	
5.	SCHEDULED EVENTS AND REMINDERS:
*	
*	
*	
*	
FOR SUPPER TONIGHT WE'LL HAVE:	
MY GOALS FOR THIS WEEK:	MY GOALS FOR THIS MONTH:

TODAY'S DATE _____

Good is the enemy of great.

Jim Collins

MY GOALS FOR TODAY:	CALLS AND CONTACTS TO MAKE TODAY:
1.	
2.	
3.	
4.	
5.	SCHEDULED EVENTS AND REMINDERS:
*	
*	
*	
*	
FOR SUPPER TONIGHT WE'LL HAVE:	
MY ULTIMATE GOAL FOR THIS YEAR:	NOTES:

TODAY'S DATE _____

Resentment is like drinking poison and then
hoping it will kill your enemies.

Nelson Mandela

MY GOALS FOR TODAY:	CALLS AND CONTACTS TO MAKE TODAY:
1.	
2.	
3.	
4.	
5.	SCHEDULED EVENTS AND REMINDERS:
*	
*	
*	
*	
FOR SUPPER TONIGHT WE'LL HAVE:	
MY GOALS FOR THIS WEEK:	MY GOALS FOR THIS MONTH:

TODAY'S DATE _____

None of us can change our yesterdays,
but all of us can change our tomorrows.

Colin Powell

MY GOALS FOR TODAY:	CALLS AND CONTACTS TO MAKE TODAY:
1.	
2.	
3.	
4.	
5.	SCHEDULED EVENTS AND REMINDERS:
*	
*	
*	
*	
FOR SUPPER TONIGHT WE'LL HAVE:	
MY ULTIMATE GOAL FOR THIS YEAR:	NOTES:

TODAY'S DATE _____

*It's easy to be negative and unmotivated,
but it takes some work to be positive and motivated.*

Donna Cardillo

MY GOALS FOR TODAY:	CALLS AND CONTACTS TO MAKE TODAY:
1.	
2.	
3.	
4.	
5.	SCHEDULED EVENTS AND REMINDERS:
*	
*	
*	
*	
FOR SUPPER TONIGHT WE'LL HAVE:	
MY GOALS FOR THIS WEEK:	MY GOALS FOR THIS MONTH:

TODAY'S DATE _____

Inspirations never go in for long engagements.
They demand immediate marriage to action.

Brendan Francis

MY GOALS FOR TODAY:	CALLS AND CONTACTS TO MAKE TODAY:
1.	
2.	
3.	
4.	
5.	SCHEDULED EVENTS AND REMINDERS:
*	
*	
*	
*	
FOR SUPPER TONIGHT WE'LL HAVE:	
MY ULTIMATE GOAL FOR THIS YEAR:	NOTES:

TODAY'S DATE _____

*The only thing that is ever foolish about
a dream is not to act on it.*

Pat Croce

MY GOALS FOR TODAY:	CALLS AND CONTACTS TO MAKE TODAY:
1.	
2.	
3.	
4.	
5.	SCHEDULED EVENTS AND REMINDERS:
*	
*	
*	
*	
FOR SUPPER TONIGHT WE'LL HAVE:	
MY GOALS FOR THIS WEEK:	MY GOALS FOR THIS MONTH:

TODAY'S DATE _____

There are times when life surprises one, and anything may happen, even what one had hoped for.

Ellen Glasgow

MY GOALS FOR TODAY:	CALLS AND CONTACTS TO MAKE TODAY:
1.	
2.	
3.	
4.	
5.	SCHEDULED EVENTS AND REMINDERS:
*	
*	
*	
*	
FOR SUPPER TONIGHT WE'LL HAVE:	
MY ULTIMATE GOAL FOR THIS YEAR:	NOTES:

TODAY'S DATE _____

None of us can live without a vision for our future.
If we don't have one, we flounder aimlessly.

Stormie Omartian

MY GOALS FOR TODAY:	CALLS AND CONTACTS TO MAKE TODAY:
1.	
2.	
3.	
4.	
5.	SCHEDULED EVENTS AND REMINDERS:
*	
*	
*	
*	
FOR SUPPER TONIGHT WE'LL HAVE:	
MY GOALS FOR THIS WEEK:	MY GOALS FOR THIS MONTH:

TODAY'S DATE _____

Is not this the true romantic feeling — not to desire to escape life,
but to prevent life from escaping you?

Thomas Wolfe

MY GOALS FOR TODAY:	CALLS AND CONTACTS TO MAKE TODAY:
1.	
2.	
3.	
4.	
5.	SCHEDULED EVENTS AND REMINDERS:
*	
*	
*	
*	
FOR SUPPER TONIGHT WE'LL HAVE:	
MY ULTIMATE GOAL FOR THIS YEAR:	NOTES:

TODAY'S DATE _____

To love oneself is the beginning of a lifelong romance.

Oscar Wilde

MY GOALS FOR TODAY:	CALLS AND CONTACTS TO MAKE TODAY:
1.	
2.	
3.	
4.	
5.	SCHEDULED EVENTS AND REMINDERS:
*	
*	
*	
*	
FOR SUPPER TONIGHT WE'LL HAVE:	
MY GOALS FOR THIS WEEK:	MY GOALS FOR THIS MONTH:

TODAY'S DATE _____

We are what we repeatedly do.

Aristotle

MY GOALS FOR TODAY:	CALLS AND CONTACTS TO MAKE TODAY:
1.	
2.	
3.	
4.	
5.	SCHEDULED EVENTS AND REMINDERS:
*	
*	
*	
*	
FOR SUPPER TONIGHT WE'LL HAVE:	
MY ULTIMATE GOAL FOR THIS YEAR:	NOTES:

TODAY'S DATE _____

We will only understand the miracle of life fully
when we allow the unexpected to happen.

Paul Coelho

MY GOALS FOR TODAY:	CALLS AND CONTACTS TO MAKE TODAY:
1.	
2.	
3.	
4.	
5.	SCHEDULED EVENTS AND REMINDERS:
*	
*	
*	
*	
FOR SUPPER TONIGHT WE'LL HAVE:	
MY GOALS FOR THIS WEEK:	MY GOALS FOR THIS MONTH:

TODAY'S DATE _____

Our journey begins by asking questions,
putting words to the movement of the heart.

The Sacred Romance

MY GOALS FOR TODAY:	CALLS AND CONTACTS TO MAKE TODAY:
1.	
2.	
3.	
4.	
5.	SCHEDULED EVENTS AND REMINDERS:
*	
*	
*	
*	
FOR SUPPER TONIGHT WE'LL HAVE:	
MY ULTIMATE GOAL FOR THIS YEAR:	NOTES:

TODAY'S DATE _____

No eye has seen, no ear has heard, no mind has conceived what
God has prepared for those who love him.

1 Corinthians 2:9

MY GOALS FOR TODAY:	CALLS AND CONTACTS TO MAKE TODAY:
1.	
2.	
3.	
4.	
5.	SCHEDULED EVENTS AND REMINDERS:
*	
*	
*	
*	
FOR SUPPER TONIGHT WE'LL HAVE:	
MY GOALS FOR THIS WEEK:	MY GOALS FOR THIS MONTH:

TODAY'S DATE _____

I have all the good qualities and resources
within me to fulfill my desires.

Lucia Capacchione

MY GOALS FOR TODAY:	CALLS AND CONTACTS TO MAKE TODAY:
1.	
2.	
3.	
4.	
5.	SCHEDULED EVENTS AND REMINDERS:
*	
*	
*	
*	
FOR SUPPER TONIGHT WE'LL HAVE:	
MY ULTIMATE GOAL FOR THIS YEAR:	NOTES:

TODAY'S DATE _____

"Come to the edge," he said. They said: "We are afraid." "Come to the edge," he said.
They came. He pushed them . . . and they flew.

Guillaume Apollinaire

MY GOALS FOR TODAY:	CALLS AND CONTACTS TO MAKE TODAY:
1.	
2.	
3.	
4.	
5.	SCHEDULED EVENTS AND REMINDERS:
*	
*	
*	
*	
FOR SUPPER TONIGHT WE'LL HAVE:	
MY GOALS FOR THIS WEEK:	MY GOALS FOR THIS MONTH:

TODAY'S DATE _____

Women trust and act upon their instincts when it concerns their children's well-being, but then shut down their sense of knowing when it's about their own needs.

Sarah Ban Breathnach

MY GOALS FOR TODAY:	CALLS AND CONTACTS TO MAKE TODAY:
1.	
2.	
3.	
4.	
5.	SCHEDULED EVENTS AND REMINDERS:
*	
*	
*	
*	
FOR SUPPER TONIGHT WE'LL HAVE:	
MY ULTIMATE GOAL FOR THIS YEAR:	NOTES:

TODAY'S DATE _____

Silence is a true friend who never betrays.

Pythagoras

MY GOALS FOR TODAY:	CALLS AND CONTACTS TO MAKE TODAY:
1.	
2.	
3.	
4.	
5.	SCHEDULED EVENTS AND REMINDERS:
*	
*	
*	
*	
FOR SUPPER TONIGHT WE'LL HAVE:	
MY GOALS FOR THIS WEEK:	MY GOALS FOR THIS MONTH:

TODAY'S DATE _____

The beginnings of all things are small.

Cicero

MY GOALS FOR TODAY:	CALLS AND CONTACTS TO MAKE TODAY:
1.	
2.	
3.	
4.	
5.	SCHEDULED EVENTS AND REMINDERS:
*	
*	
*	
*	
FOR SUPPER TONIGHT WE'LL HAVE:	
MY ULTIMATE GOAL FOR THIS YEAR:	NOTES:

NOVEMBER

This is the month for thanks and praise.
On the horizon are the holidays. Clean the house and stock the larder.
But don't you dare become a martyr.
This month EVERYONE must help Mother.
Father, Sister and even Brother.

1	
2	
3	
4	
5	
6	
7	
8	
9	
10	
11	
12	
13	
14	
15	
16	
17	
18	
19	
20	

21	
22	
23	
24	
25	
26	
27	
28	
29	
30	

FUN THINGS TO DO THIS MONTH:

1. In 1990, President George H.W. Bush approved this month to be National American Indian Heritage Month, known also as Native American Heritage Month. This is a great time to study and learn about the Natives who once reigned in the area where you now live. Many of our rivers, cities and states are named after these noble people.
2. Start Christmas shopping this month. Make it a more pleasurable experience by staying away from large department stores and visiting small boutiques and unique shops instead. Not only will you have more fun shopping, but the recipients on your list will be thrilled with their special gifts.
3. This is a great month to start a "Gratitude Journal." Every morning when you awaken or each night before going to sleep, think of five things you are grateful for and write them in your journal. (Encourage kids to do the same.) The night before Thanksgiving Day read all of your entries. It will put the THANKS into Thanksgiving.
4. Victorian women cleaned their homes until they were spotless during November to get ready for the upcoming holiday season. Try taking on one room per week, by getting rid of any items that aren't useful or beautiful. This month's donations will mean more to those less fortunate because of the upcoming holidays.

MUST DO THIS MONTH

1. I will work on this character trait during November.

_____

2. I will work on these goals this month:

_____

TODAY'S DATE _____

The world cares very little about what a man or woman knows;
it is what the man or woman is able to do that counts.

Booker T. Washington

MY GOALS FOR TODAY:	CALLS AND CONTACTS TO MAKE TODAY:
1.	
2.	
3.	
4.	
5.	SCHEDULED EVENTS AND REMINDERS:
*	
*	
*	
*	
FOR SUPPER TONIGHT WE'LL HAVE:	
MY GOALS FOR THIS WEEK:	MY GOALS FOR THIS MONTH:

TODAY'S DATE _____

No one would remember the Good Samaritan
if he'd only had good intentions.

Margaret Thatcher

MY GOALS FOR TODAY:	CALLS AND CONTACTS TO MAKE TODAY:
1.	
2.	
3.	
4.	
5.	SCHEDULED EVENTS AND REMINDERS:
*	
*	
*	
*	
FOR SUPPER TONIGHT WE'LL HAVE:	
MY ULTIMATE GOAL FOR THIS YEAR:	NOTES:

TODAY'S DATE _____

Love is a fruit that is always in season.

Mother Teresa

MY GOALS FOR TODAY:	CALLS AND CONTACTS TO MAKE TODAY:
1.	
2.	
3.	
4.	
5.	SCHEDULED EVENTS AND REMINDERS:
*	
*	
*	
*	
FOR SUPPER TONIGHT WE'LL HAVE:	
MY GOALS FOR THIS WEEK:	MY GOALS FOR THIS MONTH:

TODAY'S DATE _____

Our attitude toward life determines life's attitude toward us.

Earl Nightingale

MY GOALS FOR TODAY:	CALLS AND CONTACTS TO MAKE TODAY:
1.	
2.	
3.	
4.	
5.	SCHEDULED EVENTS AND REMINDERS:
*	
*	
*	
*	
FOR SUPPER TONIGHT WE'LL HAVE:	
MY ULTIMATE GOAL FOR THIS YEAR:	NOTES:

TODAY'S DATE _____

*What you do today is important because you are
exchanging a day of your life for it.*

Unknown

MY GOALS FOR TODAY:	CALLS AND CONTACTS TO MAKE TODAY:
1.	
2.	
3.	
4.	
5.	SCHEDULED EVENTS AND REMINDERS:
*	
*	
*	
*	
FOR SUPPER TONIGHT WE'LL HAVE:	
MY GOALS FOR THIS WEEK:	MY GOALS FOR THIS MONTH:

TODAY'S DATE _____

*All our dreams come true if — we have
the courage to pursue them.*

Walt Disney

MY GOALS FOR TODAY:	CALLS AND CONTACTS TO MAKE TODAY:
1.	
2.	
3.	
4.	
5.	SCHEDULED EVENTS AND REMINDERS:
*	
*	
*	
*	
FOR SUPPER TONIGHT WE'LL HAVE:	
MY ULTIMATE GOAL FOR THIS YEAR:	NOTES:

TODAY'S DATE _____

Even a mistake may turn out to be the one thing
necessary to worthwhile achievement.

Henry Ford

MY GOALS FOR TODAY:	CALLS AND CONTACTS TO MAKE TODAY:
1.	
2.	
3.	
4.	
5.	SCHEDULED EVENTS AND REMINDERS:
*	
*	
*	
*	
FOR SUPPER TONIGHT WE'LL HAVE:	
MY GOALS FOR THIS WEEK:	MY GOALS FOR THIS MONTH:

TODAY'S DATE _____

Believe in yourself and there will come a day when others
have no choice but to believe with you.

Cynthia Kersey

MY GOALS FOR TODAY:	CALLS AND CONTACTS TO MAKE TODAY:
1.	
2.	
3.	
4.	
5.	SCHEDULED EVENTS AND REMINDERS:
*	
*	
*	
*	
FOR SUPPER TONIGHT WE'LL HAVE:	
MY ULTIMATE GOAL FOR THIS YEAR:	NOTES:

TODAY'S DATE _____

The best years of your life are the ones in which you decide your
problems are you own. You do not blame them
on your mother, the ecology or the president.
You realize that you control your own destiny.

Albert Ellis

MY GOALS FOR TODAY:	CALLS AND CONTACTS TO MAKE TODAY:
1.	
2.	
3.	
4.	
5.	SCHEDULED EVENTS AND REMINDERS:
*	
*	
*	
*	
FOR SUPPER TONIGHT WE'LL HAVE:	
MY GOALS FOR THIS WEEK:	MY GOALS FOR THIS MONTH:

TODAY'S DATE _____

Don't say you don't have enough time. You have exactly the same amount of hours per day that were given to Helen Keller, Pasteur, Michelangelo, Mother Teresa, Thomas Jefferson, and Albert Einstein.

H. Jackson Brown, Jr.

MY GOALS FOR TODAY:	CALLS AND CONTACTS TO MAKE TODAY:
1.	
2.	
3.	
4.	
5.	SCHEDULED EVENTS AND REMINDERS:
*	
*	
*	
*	
FOR SUPPER TONIGHT WE'LL HAVE:	
MY ULTIMATE GOAL FOR THIS YEAR:	NOTES:

TODAY'S DATE _____

Have the courage to follow your heart and intuition. They somehow already know what you truly want to become.

Steve Jobs

MY GOALS FOR TODAY:	CALLS AND CONTACTS TO MAKE TODAY:
1.	
2.	
3.	
4.	
5.	SCHEDULED EVENTS AND REMINDERS:
*	
*	
*	
*	
FOR SUPPER TONIGHT WE'LL HAVE:	
MY GOALS FOR THIS WEEK:	MY GOALS FOR THIS MONTH:

TODAY'S DATE _____

When you can't change the direction of the
wind — adjust your sails.

H. Jackson Brown

MY GOALS FOR TODAY:	CALLS AND CONTACTS TO MAKE TODAY:
1.	
2.	
3.	
4.	
5.	SCHEDULED EVENTS AND REMINDERS:
*	
*	
*	
*	
FOR SUPPER TONIGHT WE'LL HAVE:	
MY ULTIMATE GOAL FOR THIS YEAR:	NOTES:

TODAY'S DATE _____

You can practice any virtue, but nothing
consistently without courage.

Maya Angelou

MY GOALS FOR TODAY:	CALLS AND CONTACTS TO MAKE TODAY:
1.	
2.	
3.	
4.	
5.	SCHEDULED EVENTS AND REMINDERS:
*	
*	
*	
*	
FOR SUPPER TONIGHT WE'LL HAVE:	
MY GOALS FOR THIS WEEK:	MY GOALS FOR THIS MONTH:

TODAY'S DATE _____

The trouble with not having a goal is that you spend your life running up and down the field and never score.

Bill Copeland

MY GOALS FOR TODAY:	CALLS AND CONTACTS TO MAKE TODAY:
1.	
2.	
3.	
4.	
5.	SCHEDULED EVENTS AND REMINDERS:
*	
*	
*	
*	
FOR SUPPER TONIGHT WE'LL HAVE:	
MY ULTIMATE GOAL FOR THIS YEAR:	NOTES:

TODAY'S DATE _____

Great minds discuss ideas. Average minds discuss events.
Small minds discuss people.

Eleanor Roosevelt

MY GOALS FOR TODAY:	CALLS AND CONTACTS TO MAKE TODAY:
1.	
2.	
3.	
4.	
5.	SCHEDULED EVENTS AND REMINDERS:
*	
*	
*	
*	
FOR SUPPER TONIGHT WE'LL HAVE:	
MY GOALS FOR THIS WEEK:	MY GOALS FOR THIS MONTH:

TODAY'S DATE _____

A journey is like a marriage. The certain way to be wrong is to think you control it.

John Steinbeck

MY GOALS FOR TODAY:	CALLS AND CONTACTS TO MAKE TODAY:
1.	
2.	
3.	
4.	
5.	SCHEDULED EVENTS AND REMINDERS:
*	
*	
*	
*	
FOR SUPPER TONIGHT WE'LL HAVE:	
MY ULTIMATE GOAL FOR THIS YEAR:	NOTES:

TODAY'S DATE _____

I've believed as many as six impossible things before breakfast.
                                                    Lewis Carroll

MY GOALS FOR TODAY:	CALLS AND CONTACTS TO MAKE TODAY:
1.	
2.	
3.	
4.	
5.	SCHEDULED EVENTS AND REMINDERS:
*	
*	
*	
*	
FOR SUPPER TONIGHT WE'LL HAVE:	
MY GOALS FOR THIS WEEK:	MY GOALS FOR THIS MONTH:

TODAY'S DATE _____

You will find the key to success under the alarm clock.

Benjamin Franklin

MY GOALS FOR TODAY:	CALLS AND CONTACTS TO MAKE TODAY:
1.	
2.	
3.	
4.	
5.	SCHEDULED EVENTS AND REMINDERS:
*	
*	
*	
*	
FOR SUPPER TONIGHT WE'LL HAVE:	
MY ULTIMATE GOAL FOR THIS YEAR:	NOTES:

TODAY'S DATE _____

Flaming enthusiasm, backed by horse sense and persistence,
is the quality that most frequently makes for success.

Dale Carnegie

MY GOALS FOR TODAY:	CALLS AND CONTACTS TO MAKE TODAY:
1.	
2.	
3.	
4.	
5.	SCHEDULED EVENTS AND REMINDERS:
*	
*	
*	
*	
FOR SUPPER TONIGHT WE'LL HAVE:	
MY GOALS FOR THIS WEEK:	MY GOALS FOR THIS MONTH:

TODAY'S DATE _____

We may assume nothing great in the world
has been accomplished without passion.

Hegel

MY GOALS FOR TODAY:	CALLS AND CONTACTS TO MAKE TODAY:
1.	
2.	
3.	
4.	
5.	SCHEDULED EVENTS AND REMINDERS:
*	
*	
*	
*	
FOR SUPPER TONIGHT WE'LL HAVE:	
MY ULTIMATE GOAL FOR THIS YEAR:	NOTES:

TODAY'S DATE _____

Looking for God is like seeking a path in a field of snow; if
there is no path and you are looking for one,
walk across it and there is your path.

Thomas Merton

MY GOALS FOR TODAY:	CALLS AND CONTACTS TO MAKE TODAY:
1.	
2.	
3.	
4.	
5.	SCHEDULED EVENTS AND REMINDERS:
*	
*	
*	
*	
FOR SUPPER TONIGHT WE'LL HAVE:	
MY GOALS FOR THIS WEEK:	MY GOALS FOR THIS MONTH:

TODAY'S DATE _____

Forgive others. Do it not only for their sake, but for your own. If you don't, you will feel within you a nauseating resentment, destroying you from within.

Maxwell Maltz

MY GOALS FOR TODAY:	CALLS AND CONTACTS TO MAKE TODAY:
1.	
2.	
3.	
4.	
5.	SCHEDULED EVENTS AND REMINDERS:
*	
*	
*	
*	
FOR SUPPER TONIGHT WE'LL HAVE:	
MY ULTIMATE GOAL FOR THIS YEAR:	NOTES:

DECEMBER

Time set aside to celebrate Christ's birth. Heaven comes closer to our earth.
With colors everywhere: gold, silver, green and red.
Wonderful greetings must be spread.
This month has the longest night – but Christmas comes with dawn's new Light.

1	
2	
3	
4	
5	
6	
7	
8	
9	
10	
11	
12	
13	
14	
15	
16	
17	
18	
19	
20	
21	

22	
23	
24	
25	
26	
27	
28	
29	
30	
31	

FUN THINGS TO DO THIS MONTH:

1. Pick one night during this month to ride around and admire all the beautiful Christmas lights. Afterward go home and eat Christmas cookies while sipping hot chocolate and watching a beautiful Holiday movie.
2. No matter what your religious preference, *It's a Wonderful Life*, is a Christmas movie we can all learn from. Make it a tradition to watch this movie, starring the beloved Jimmy Stewart, every year to help you realize just how valuable you really are to this wonderful world.
3. Bring cheer to a couple of shut-ins this month by paying them a visit and bringing them a small gift. It can be a new kitchen towel or a plate of cookies, you decide. If you have children encourage them to go with you, everyone will be happier because of this small gesture of love and kindness.
4. Read the story, *A Christmas Carol*, by Charles Dickens to yourself. Read the story, *Small One*, by Alex Walsh to a child.
5. Look over all of the things you have accomplished this year. If you accomplished only five goals per day, only five days per week you achieved 1,300 goals. Great job! If you reached weekly and monthly goals the number is even higher. Did you achieve your ultimate goal? If so, congratulations. If not, don't stop trying. Most people give up right before success is about to be achieved. A new year needs a new plan. Shall we begin?

MUST DO THIS MONTH

1. I will work on this character trait in December.

2. I will work on these goals this month:

TODAY'S DATE _____

Never look down on anybody unless you're helping him up.

Jesse Jackson

MY GOALS FOR TODAY:	CALLS AND CONTACTS TO MAKE TODAY:
1.	
2.	
3.	
4.	
5.	SCHEDULED EVENTS AND REMINDERS:
*	
*	
*	
*	
FOR SUPPER TONIGHT WE'LL HAVE:	
MY GOALS FOR THIS WEEK:	MY GOALS FOR THIS MONTH:

TODAY'S DATE _____

Genius is the ability to put into effect what is on your mind.

F. Scott Fitzgerald

MY GOALS FOR TODAY:	CALLS AND CONTACTS TO MAKE TODAY:
1.	
2.	
3.	
4.	
5.	SCHEDULED EVENTS AND REMINDERS:
*	
*	
*	
*	
FOR SUPPER TONIGHT WE'LL HAVE:	
MY ULTIMATE GOAL FOR THIS YEAR:	NOTES:

TODAY'S DATE _____

When you live in constant communion with God,
you cannot be lonely . . .

Peace Pilgrim

MY GOALS FOR TODAY:	CALLS AND CONTACTS TO MAKE TODAY:
1.	
2.	
3.	
4.	
5.	SCHEDULED EVENTS AND REMINDERS:
*	
*	
*	
*	
FOR SUPPER TONIGHT WE'LL HAVE:	
MY GOALS FOR THIS WEEK:	MY GOALS FOR THIS MONTH:

TODAY'S DATE _____

A man who cannot tolerate small ills can never accomplish great things.

Chinese proverb

MY GOALS FOR TODAY:	CALLS AND CONTACTS TO MAKE TODAY:
1.	
2.	
3.	
4.	
5.	SCHEDULED EVENTS AND REMINDERS:
*	
*	
*	
*	
FOR SUPPER TONIGHT WE'LL HAVE:	
MY ULTIMATE GOAL FOR THIS YEAR:	NOTES:

TODAY'S DATE _____

God loves a cheerful giver. She gives most who gives with joy.
Mother Teresa

MY GOALS FOR TODAY:	CALLS AND CONTACTS TO MAKE TODAY:
1.	
2.	
3.	
4.	
5.	SCHEDULED EVENTS AND REMINDERS:
*	
*	
*	
*	
FOR SUPPER TONIGHT WE'LL HAVE:	
MY GOALS FOR THIS WEEK:	MY GOALS FOR THIS MONTH:

TODAY'S DATE _____

Be generous, not wasteful; give, not indiscriminately . . .

Mahabharata

MY GOALS FOR TODAY:	CALLS AND CONTACTS TO MAKE TODAY:
1.	
2.	
3.	
4.	
5.	SCHEDULED EVENTS AND REMINDERS:
*	
*	
*	
*	
FOR SUPPER TONIGHT WE'LL HAVE:	
MY ULTIMATE GOAL FOR THIS YEAR:	NOTES:

TODAY'S DATE _____

Most of the joy of living comes out of
true giving — giving without strings attached . . .

Gary Emery

MY GOALS FOR TODAY:	CALLS AND CONTACTS TO MAKE TODAY:
1.	
2.	
3.	
4.	
5.	SCHEDULED EVENTS AND REMINDERS:
*	
*	
*	
*	
FOR SUPPER TONIGHT WE'LL HAVE:	
MY GOALS FOR THIS WEEK:	MY GOALS FOR THIS MONTH:

TODAY'S DATE _____

Every gift, though it be small,
is in reality great if given with affection . . .

Pindar

MY GOALS FOR TODAY:	CALLS AND CONTACTS TO MAKE TODAY:
1.	
2.	
3.	
4.	
5.	SCHEDULED EVENTS AND REMINDERS:
*	
*	
*	
*	
FOR SUPPER TONIGHT WE'LL HAVE:	
MY ULTIMATE GOAL FOR THIS YEAR:	NOTES:

TODAY'S DATE _____

To receive everything, one must open one's hands and give.
                                              Taisen Deshimaru

MY GOALS FOR TODAY:	CALLS AND CONTACTS TO MAKE TODAY:
1.	
2.	
3.	
4.	
5.	SCHEDULED EVENTS AND REMINDERS:
*	
*	
*	
*	
FOR SUPPER TONIGHT WE'LL HAVE:	
MY GOALS FOR THIS WEEK:	MY GOALS FOR THIS MONTH:

TODAY'S DATE _____

He that falls in love with himself will have no rivals. . .

Benjamin Franklin

MY GOALS FOR TODAY:	CALLS AND CONTACTS TO MAKE TODAY:
1.	
2.	
3.	
4.	
5.	SCHEDULED EVENTS AND REMINDERS:
*	
*	
*	
*	
FOR SUPPER TONIGHT WE'LL HAVE:	
MY ULTIMATE GOAL FOR THIS YEAR:	NOTES:

TODAY'S DATE _____

One of ego's favorite paths of resistance
is to fill you with doubt . . .

Ram Dass

MY GOALS FOR TODAY:	CALLS AND CONTACTS TO MAKE TODAY:
1.	
2.	
3.	
4.	
5.	SCHEDULED EVENTS AND REMINDERS:
*	
*	
*	
*	
FOR SUPPER TONIGHT WE'LL HAVE:	
MY GOALS FOR THIS WEEK:	MY GOALS FOR THIS MONTH:

TODAY'S DATE _____

A bit of fragrance always clings to the hand that gives you roses . . .

Chinese proverb

MY GOALS FOR TODAY:	CALLS AND CONTACTS TO MAKE TODAY:
1.	
2.	
3.	
4.	
5.	SCHEDULED EVENTS AND REMINDERS:
*	
*	
*	
*	
FOR SUPPER TONIGHT WE'LL HAVE:	
MY ULTIMATE GOAL FOR THIS YEAR:	NOTES:

TODAY'S DATE _____

Do not worry about tomorrow; it will have enough worries of its own. There is no need to add to the troubles each day brings
Jesus

MY GOALS FOR TODAY:	CALLS AND CONTACTS TO MAKE TODAY:
1.	
2.	
3.	
4.	
5.	SCHEDULED EVENTS AND REMINDERS:
*	
*	
*	
*	
FOR SUPPER TONIGHT WE'LL HAVE:	
MY GOALS FOR THIS WEEK:	MY GOALS FOR THIS MONTH:

TODAY'S DATE _____

Beware of dissipating your powers;
strive constantly to concentrate them.

Johann W. Goethe

MY GOALS FOR TODAY:	CALLS AND CONTACTS TO MAKE TODAY:
1.	
2.	
3.	
4.	
5.	SCHEDULED EVENTS AND REMINDERS:
*	
*	
*	
*	
FOR SUPPER TONIGHT WE'LL HAVE:	
MY ULTIMATE GOAL FOR THIS YEAR:	NOTES:

TODAY'S DATE _____

*Our supreme goal should be a state of mind in which invisible
things are of more importance than the visible.*

Alice H. Rice

MY GOALS FOR TODAY:	CALLS AND CONTACTS TO MAKE TODAY:
1.	
2.	
3.	
4.	
5.	SCHEDULED EVENTS AND REMINDERS:
*	
*	
*	
*	
FOR SUPPER TONIGHT WE'LL HAVE:	
MY GOALS FOR THIS WEEK:	MY GOALS FOR THIS MONTH:

TODAY'S DATE _____

If you have no goals, your thoughts will take you
toward what you think about most.

Andrew Matthews

MY GOALS FOR TODAY:	CALLS AND CONTACTS TO MAKE TODAY:
1.	
2.	
3.	
4.	
5.	SCHEDULED EVENTS AND REMINDERS:
*	
*	
*	
*	
FOR SUPPER TONIGHT WE'LL HAVE:	
MY ULTIMATE GOAL FOR THIS YEAR:	NOTES:

TODAY'S DATE _____

> *The reason most people never reach their goals
> is that they don't define them, or ever seriously
> consider them as believable or achievable.*
>
> Denis Waitley

MY GOALS FOR TODAY:	CALLS AND CONTACTS TO MAKE TODAY:
1.	
2.	
3.	
4.	
5.	SCHEDULED EVENTS AND REMINDERS:
*	
*	
*	
*	
FOR SUPPER TONIGHT WE'LL HAVE:	
MY GOALS FOR THIS WEEK:	MY GOALS FOR THIS MONTH:

TODAY'S DATE _____

Many persons have the wrong idea of what constitutes true
happiness. It is not attained through self-gratification but
through fidelity to a worthy purpose.

Helen Keller

MY GOALS FOR TODAY:	CALLS AND CONTACTS TO MAKE TODAY:
1.	
2.	
3.	
4.	
5.	SCHEDULED EVENTS AND REMINDERS:
*	
*	
*	
*	
FOR SUPPER TONIGHT WE'LL HAVE:	
MY ULTIMATE GOAL FOR THIS YEAR:	NOTES:

TODAY'S DATE _____

*Not having a goal is more to fear
than not reaching a goal.*

Robert Schuller

MY GOALS FOR TODAY:	CALLS AND CONTACTS TO MAKE TODAY:
1.	
2.	
3.	
4.	
5.	SCHEDULED EVENTS AND REMINDERS:
*	
*	
*	
*	
FOR SUPPER TONIGHT WE'LL HAVE:	
MY GOALS FOR THIS WEEK:	MY GOALS FOR THIS MONTH:

TODAY'S DATE _____

You must have long-range goals to keep you
from being frustrated by short-range failure.

Charles C. Noble

MY GOALS FOR TODAY:	CALLS AND CONTACTS TO MAKE TODAY:
1.	
2.	
3.	
4.	
5.	SCHEDULED EVENTS AND REMINDERS:
*	
*	
*	
*	
FOR SUPPER TONIGHT WE'LL HAVE:	
MY ULTIMATE GOAL FOR THIS YEAR:	NOTES:

TODAY'S DATE _____

Love is the great solvent of all difficulties,
all problems, all misunderstandings.

White Eagle

MY GOALS FOR TODAY:	CALLS AND CONTACTS TO MAKE TODAY:
1.	
2.	
3.	
4.	
5.	SCHEDULED EVENTS AND REMINDERS:
*	
*	
*	
*	
FOR SUPPER TONIGHT WE'LL HAVE:	
MY GOALS FOR THIS WEEK:	MY GOALS FOR THIS MONTH:

TODAY'S DATE _____

Contentment is the Philosopher's stone,
that turns all it touches to gold.

Benjamin Franklin

MY GOALS FOR TODAY:	CALLS AND CONTACTS TO MAKE TODAY:
1.	
2.	
3.	
4.	
5.	SCHEDULED EVENTS AND REMINDERS:
*	
*	
*	
*	
FOR SUPPER TONIGHT WE'LL HAVE:	
MY ULTIMATE GOAL FOR THIS YEAR:	NOTES:

TODAY'S DATE _____

Anything unattempted remains impossible.

Unknown

MY GOALS FOR TODAY:	CALLS AND CONTACTS TO MAKE TODAY:
1.	
2.	
3.	
4.	
5.	SCHEDULED EVENTS AND REMINDERS:
*	
*	
*	
*	
FOR SUPPER TONIGHT WE'LL HAVE:	
MY GOALS FOR THIS WEEK:	MY GOALS FOR THIS MONTH:

TODAY'S DATE _____

They can conquer who believe they can.

Virgil

MY GOALS FOR TODAY:	CALLS AND CONTACTS TO MAKE TODAY:
1.	
2.	
3.	
4.	
5.	SCHEDULED EVENTS AND REMINDERS:
*	
*	
*	
*	
FOR SUPPER TONIGHT WE'LL HAVE:	
MY ULTIMATE GOAL FOR THIS YEAR:	NOTES:

TO ACCOMPLISH LARGER GOALS:

Socrates tells us, "Let him that would move the world first move himself." This is some good advice, but in what direction should we move? Most of the time, it's much easier to do something if you have detailed directions on what to do and in the order in which to carry them through. Since life doesn't really come with instruction sheets, you must design them yourself, to fit the intended goal. One of the best things to start with is a sharp pencil, an eraser, and a sheet of paper. I prefer lined notebook paper.

Example:

Step 1. Write the desired goal at the top of the page.

Buy a new house   .

Step 2. Now decide exactly what it is you must do – to buy that new home. At this point there is no order. Just start writing.

Decide on a location   .

Look online to find homes of interest   .

Find a trust-worthy realtor   .

Start packing up things in our home   .

Decide on a price range   .

Decide what to do with our house   .

This list, of course, is not complete, but you get the idea. Keep writing until you cannot think of anything else.

Step 3. Go over your list. What seems to be the first five things of importance. Highlight them. Now decide what to do first and put it in your, *MY GOALS FOR THIS WEEK* or *MY GOALS FOR THIS MONTH*, depending on how much time you have to set aside to make this step happen.

Step 4. Cross off each item on your list as you complete it. I prefer to do this step in red. It is important to do this in a different color, so when you glance at your list, you know immediately what is already accomplished.

Step 5. Repeat process over and over again, until you have achieved your goal.

You may have to have more than one sheet of paper going at once. One for the actions you, yourself must do. One for the questions you have for your realtor, banker, etc. Keep these lists in separate files or one folder; this is a matter of preference. Inside your folders keep anything of importance that might be helpful to refer to later.

Always remember the words of Napoleon Hill:

"I know that I have the ability to achieve the object of my Definite Purpose in life, therefore, I demand of myself persistent, continuous action toward its attainment, and I here and now promise to render such action."

Only five steps to take over and over again until you reach your dream. It's not as hard as you think. Now, what is it that you want to achieve? Begin it now by moving in the right direction. What are you waiting for? Now, you even have instructions. ☺

Congratulations! You have just completed over **1,300** goals! This is a spectacular accomplishment by anyone's standard. Pat yourself on the back and be proud of the year you've lived. You are wonderful! You are an achiever.

I would love to hear about all you've accomplished. Please let me know what you've done. Post it on my website at www.laurahuber.com.

www.ingramcontent.com/pod-product-compliance
Lightning Source LLC
Chambersburg PA
CBHW022114080426
42734CB00006B/131